The Crucifixion

and

The Resurrection

of

JESUS

BY AN EYE-WITNESS

A discovered MSS. of the old Alexandria Library giving,
almost complete, a remarkable and lengthy letter,
full, detailed, graphic and apparently truthful
account by an Eye-Witness and friend of
Jesus, an Elder of the Essene Order,
to which Jesus belonged, show-
ing Jesus did not die upon
the Cross but six
months later.

With much additional and explanatory matter
concerning the Essenes and the Crucifixion story.

THE AUSTIN PUBLISHING CO.
LOS ANGELES
CALIFORNIA

CONTENTS

		Page
1.	Dr. Morris' Statement	4
2.	The Story of the Essene Elder's Letter .	5
3.	The Essenes	11
4.	Statement of the German Translators of the Latin Manuscript	19
5.	The Explanation of the Three Members of the Muskegon T. S., who made the English Translation	25
6.	Scriptural Accounts of the Crucifixion . .	26
7.	The Letter of the Essene Elder . . .	40
8.	Addendum	96

Dr. Morris' Statement

In making copies of rare books and manuscripts in the Library of the Christian Israelites about fifteen years ago, I came across the MSS copy of this wonderful Letter of the Essene Elder in Jerusalem to his Brother Elder in Alexandria, and copied it as accurately as I could. The treasured wisdom in this and similar libraries of this Order is not available for the public, and only accessible to advanced students for their private study and benefit and not to be given broadcast to the world, the theory being held that only the initiated can properly interpret and use occult lore and that men will seek such wisdom as soon as they are capable of making good use of it.

Despite these teachings, however, I have become so deeply impressed with the importance of this letter and the great interest it will undoubtedly excite among scholars and Bible students the world over, that I have had no hesitation in handing it over to Dr. Austin for publication.

DR. ELSIE LOUISE MORRIS.
229 Alexandria St., Los Angeles.
February 1st, 1919.

The Story of the Essene Elder's Letter

While conversing with Dr. Elsie Louise Morris in her home, 229 Alexandria street, Los Angeles, a few months ago concerning her forthcoming book: "Woman, Past, Present and Future", which I am publishing, she showed me among many other interesting literary products, a MSS copy made by her own hand of the Essene Elder's Letter which forms the chief feature of this book. Dr. Morris will state in her own language what she knows about the manuscript from which she made her copy and the circumstances under which she made it.

On reading it I was at once struck with the simplicity and candor of the narrative, and somehow felt impressed with its essential truth, and also with the deep interest and importance which the religious world would attach to such a letter, providing it carried to other minds the same internal evidence of truth that had impressed my own.

After carefully perusing the MSS for some time, I concluded its contents would interest most deeply too large a section of humanity to allow the Essene

Letter to remain in the obscurity of private possession, or in the archives of a Secret Order. So I began negotiations with Dr. Morris and secured the "Letter", and the introductory articles by the German translators, who translated the Latin MSS into German, and by the Fellows of the Theosophical Society, who made the translation from Swedish into English.

I now propose to state briefly some of my reasons for believing in the essential truth of this story of the Crucifixion and Resuscitation of Jesus, and why I think it should be published to the world.

First, and perhaps chiefly, because the spirit and language of the "Letter" impresses every openminded reader with its truth. Language, spoken or written, has an inner voice and testimony and speaks not only to the understanding but speaks to the moral sense as well. When any lover of truth hears a speaker or reads a narrative, the soul of the speaker or writer is revealed. It is the note of sterling honesty in the voice, or in the language and style of expression, that infallibly announces the truth, as the ring of the gold coin proclaims its genuineness.

The "Letter" breathes the air and spirit of the East and is redolent of the ancient times.

It is the product of a heart in love with truth and full of reverence for all that is good and beautiful in human life and character.

The narrative is permeated throughout with that

loving, tender and self-sacrificing devotion to the Master that manifests in an unmistakable manner. It would seem impossible for this feature to spring out of any mind and heart but that of a personal follower of Jesus, bound to him with a thousand ties of tenderest affection.

The whole "Letter" may be looked upon as a commentary on the Gospel narrative ~ throwing a flood of light on much that before was obscure ~ with one great difference, viz.: an utter absence of the supernatural, the so-called miraculous element.

As, according to the story, Jesus did not die on the Cross, so his "Resurrection" was in reality a "Resuscitation", and so the whole series of events falls within the compass of natural law.

This view doubtless will be intensely objectionable to multitudes, but if it could be accepted and established as true, would at once remove the greatest objection that sceptics, infidels and scholars have urged against the Gospel narrative.

Quite true this would be ~ in the opinion of many ~ a complete demolition of the Christian Religion, since multitudes today, as in the time of Jesus, put the emphasis on the miraculous displays of power rather than on the utterance of lofty truth.

To these the death of Jesus means more than his life. Miraculous power, manifesting in signs and wonders, is much more valuable to them than the Sermon on the Mount, or the incarnation of the truth in the

Master's life.

There is absolutely nothing in the truthful story of the Crucifixion to render the death of Jesus on the Cross a necessity. In the first place only the hands were pierced, as we learn on the best authority. The suffering and danger from loss of blood and pain from the hand wounds was very much lessened by the custom of binding the arms very tightly to the Cross, partially stopping the blood circulation and benumbing the pain by pressure upon the nerves. Those crucified in other lands were allowed to remain on the cross till death resulted naturally from the crucifixion and in some cases we are told survived for a week after the infliction of the penalty. Jesus, a sensitive, that is peculiarly a sufferer, after the flogging and burdenbearing naturally swooned under the pain of the crucifixion. There is no mention in the "Letter" of any wounds in the feet, or any healing treatment applied thereto.

If Jesus were, therefore, as the "Letter" states, a member of the Order of Essenes, and befriended as far as the rules of the Order would allow any public activities in apparent opposition to the State, by members of his Order, what is more natural to suppose than that he was shielded from having his bones broken by the soldiers, and his body carefully laid away in the sepulchre of another Essene and, by arts of healing well known to the Order, restored to consciousness and to active life again?

The actual flowing of water and blood from the wound in the side is a great physiological proof that life was not extinct in his body at that time.

Again, Jesus after his resurrection as before his death, never appeared at two places at the same time. He seemed, therefore, subject to time and place like other mortals.

People believed many things in those days that seem incredible to us today. Those who could readily believe that a crucified man, dead and buried, could arise, could readily construe the departure of Jesus in a cloud overhanging Olivet and shot through with the golden rays of a setting sun, into an ascension into heaven.

The one objection that has apparent strength, presuming the "Letter" genuine and authentic and Jesus a member of the Essenes, is this: Why did Jesus, a member of the Order, pledged as such to a secluded life, and pledged also to limiting his instructions to the initiated, publicly pursue his ministry and preach to the multitude?

The answer to this is found in the fact, apparent through the whole "Letter" narrative, that Jesus through the mighty spirit inspiration that was upon him broke through the narrow limitations of the Order and made his ministry universal. So strong the compassion of his noble heart, so mighty the tide of inspiration that surged through his being, so urgent the truth that sought expression through his lips, that he was carried outside the pale of the Monastic Order into a ministry for the whole race.

"Thus we have every reason to credit this "Letter", dictated by a lover of truth, and written by a man who had been an EYE-WITNESS to most of the important transactions in the life and death of Jesus, who, as a member of the Order, was embraced by them with all the fraternal devotion of the Order."

B. F. AUSTIN.

The Essenes

The Essenes, to whom such frequent references are made in this book, were a Monastic Order among the Jews, the origin of which is lost in the obscurity of the distant past.

Pliny represents them as a perennial colony on the shores of the Dead Sea.

Philo and Josephus estimate their number at 4,000.

Undoubtedly they were mostly Jews and sprang out of the heart of Judaism, but it is equally certain they were far from orthodox Jews and there existed in the spirit and methods of the Order much that was of a foreign character and distinctly anti-Jewish.

Much variety of opinion exists among scholars and writers as to the origin of the name and great diversity of views has been expressed, especially as to the foreign and anti-Jewish elements in the teaching and practice of the Essenes.

Their first definite appearance in history is in the time of Jonathan, the Maccabee, 161-144 B. C., though many authorities give them a much earlier origin. Pliny, the Elder, speaks of them as having existed "thousands of ages", but the best scholar-ship regards this as a most extravagant expression. The writers best qualified give them a "dateless antiquity." Some explain the name Essenes as mean-ing "the silent ones", and others as signifying "the healers", and others assert the term means "the pious".

Philo, Pliny and Josephus are the chief authorities on the Essenes. Josephus, who was at one time a member of the Order, treats of them at great length.

The prevailing spirit of the Order embraced sev-ere asceticism, rare benevolence to each other and to all men, especially to the aged, the poor and the stranger. They had fixed and very rigid rules for initiation and each step of the four grades of mem-bership was won by strict compliance with discipline and strict obedience to those in authority. The life of the member was regulated by fixed rules under all circumstances.

They gained their recruits in membership in two ways: converts from the world and the adoption and rearing of orphan children. As marriage was gen-erally prohibited and denounced, there was little accession to their membership from children of the Order.

This Society is said to have been the first to denounce slavery. It practiced complete community of goods and this ~ unlike the community of goods that prevailed for a time among the early Christians and was voluntary ~ was obligatory on all joining the Order.

They chose their own Priests and Judges. There was in their teaching a considerable element of speculation and a profound sympathy with the Grecian Philosophy and with many Oriental ideas and teachings.

They had no special city of their own, but had communities in various cities and preferred the country or villages to the city life. They did not take an active part in the public life of the nation, but lived largely to themselves, devoting their chief attention to the work of the Order.

Agriculture was their favorite pursuit and hence their preference for rural life. They adopted children and reared them in the principles and practices of their Order.

Their practice in regard to dress was very ascetic. They wore their clothes and shoes until they fell away from them. Except when toiling in the fields they dressed invariably in white.

Before sunrise no one spoke a profane word. At sunrise they offered to the sun traditional forms of prayer as though beseeching it to rise. They then went to work till the fifth hour, when they assembled and girding on a linen garment, bathed in cold water. They then seated themselves in the dining hall, where the bakers placed bread before them, and the cook brought to each a single dish of food. Grace was said before and after meal by the Priest.

After dinner they resumed work till sunset. In the evening they had supper and entertained their guests.

They were a very quiet people and the visitor and stranger was impressed with awe at the tranquility of the place.

All the activities of the members were directed by the President, and in only two things were the members allowed to act upon their own initiative: They could help those in trouble and show charity to the poor. No member, however, could give anything to his own relatives, except on the authority of the heads of the Society.

They had a Special Court of Justice composed of 100 members, and its decisions were rendered with extreme care and were irreversible. Oaths were forbidden, as the ordinary promise was considered stronger.

The moral characteristics of life and conduct were most zealously cultivated.

After a novitiate of three years, during which the candidate was rigorously tested in every way, he was, if found worthy, admitted to the full membership.

Before admission and before being allowed to partake of the common meal, he was required to swear an awful oath: 1. To reverence the Deity. 2. Do justice to all men. 3. Hurt no one voluntarily, or at the command of another. 4. Hate the unjust and assist the just. 5. Faithful to all men, especially to rulers for all authority is of God. 6. Also should he himself ever bear rule, he would make no violent use of his power, nor attempt to outshine those under him by display. 7. Cherish the truth and unmask all liars. 8. Seek no unjust gain. 9. Conceal nothing from fellow members. 10. Not divulge the affairs of the Society. 11. Transmit to others the teachings of the Society unchanged. 12. Keep sacred the books of the Society. 13. Not reveal the names of the angels.

Members guilty of any crime were, on conviction, expelled from the order.

While this Monastic Order, fenced off from the world most carefully, arose out of the heart of Judaism and most of its membership were Jews, it is also interesting to note the ~

Many Sharp Lines of Distinction Between Essenism and Orthodox Judaism

1. The Essenes did not offer animal sacrifices.
2. They prohibited slaughter and the eating of flesh.
3. They held marriage in low estimation and allowed it in exceptional cases, but only for purposes of procreation.
4. The Essenes addressed prayers and invocations to the sun.
5. There was no such rigid asceticism among the

Jews as the Essenes practiced, discarding as they did warm baths and looking upon oil, even that used for anointment, as defilement.

Some of St. Paul's views of marriage, it must be confessed, were kindred to those of the Essenes.

If the Essenes as a community had a central location the shores of the Dead Sea may be so regarded.

The Foreign Element in Essenism

Dr. Lightfoot, an eminent authority on "The Apostolic Age," holds the view that the Foreign Element in Essenism is traceable to Medo-Persian teaching. Among his reasons are the following:

1. Both recognize that Dualism which forms the distinguishing feature of the Persian teaching.

2. The Essenes worshipped "the angels" and the Zendavesta teaches "the invocation of spirits."

3. Both systems recognize intermediary beings in the government of nature and of man.

4. The reverence for light, its symbolism, and the worship of the sun exists in both systems.

5. Magic was very attractive to the Essenes and extensively used by them ~ and, as we know, the very word is derived from the "Magi" or priests of the Persian religion.

6. Both systems aimed at the purification of the individual.

7. Both cults favored the white garb.

The relation of Jesus, if any, to this Order that undoubtedly flourished in Jerusalem at the time of his ministry, has been a frequent topic with students and writers.

One author declares: "It will hardly be doubted that our Saviour, himself belonged to this Order."

If the "Letter" of the Essene Elder, which forms the chief feature of this book, may be regarded as genuine, or as depicting truthfully the times in which Jesus ministered, all must regard Jesus as an Essene.

Certain it is that this would explain very many points of agreement between the teachings of the Master and those of the Essenes, yet it would leave many points of divergence in teaching and practice to be explained away.

These, however, would not appear so formidable if one heeds the hints repeatedly given in the "Letter," that while Jesus was reared by the Essenes and accepted most of their principles and practices, toward the end of his ministry he threw off and utterly rejected some of its customs and refused obedience to the Elders of the Order, acting under an inspiration of his own rather than the counsels or commands of the Order.

That the Essenes and early Christians were very similar in their belief and formal instruction may be inferred from the following facts:

1. Both taught the immortality of the soul and a future, dependent in a measure, on our conduct here.

2. Both taught and practiced community of goods.

3. Both abhorred the too common use of oaths.

4. Both taught passive obedience to authority. "The powers that be were ordained of God."

5. Neither system seemed to have the most exalted views of marriage. Compare Paul's teaching on marriage with Essenism.

6. Both exalted poverty and centered attention on spiritual rather than worldly interests.

The writer's own views are expressed in his story of the Essene Letter.

B. F. AUSTIN.

A Valuable History and Enlightenment

On the Right Manner of the Life and Death of Jesus.

Old Manuscripts which were found in Alexandria, written by one of the Essene Order to which Jesus belonged.

THE NEW EDITION
J. F. Sasberg
1880
Translated from the above named edition
(Swedish)

FOREWORD OF THE GERMAN TRANSLATORS

Through one of the members of the Abyssinian merchants' company, was found in Alexandria, in an old building, formerly used by Grecian Monks, in a forgotton and abandoned library, an old parchment roll, the deciphering of which had scarcely been begun by a learned man. A Missionary in his fanatical orthodox eagerness tried to destroy the antique document. But it was saved with the exception of a few supplements, contained in the roll, and a literal translation of the ancient Latin text was accomplished. And which transcript came to Germany through the Free-Masons.

Through the archeological researches which was prosecuted in Alexandria, even the place where it was found, it has been shown that in the far off remote times, under the sway of the Romans, and in the time of Christ it had been owned by the Essene Order, and this parchment roll is a relic from the Essene colony. The learned man who was present when it was found was a Frenchman. He sought to bring the original to the possession of the French Academy. If this did not occur it was owing to intrigue of the Catholic officials, and especially of the Jesuit Mission in Egypt, because they had from the beginning labored to destroy all trace of this document. But the true transcript through the influence of influential Abyssinian merchants and prominent Triest Commissioner was completed by the learned Frenchman and natural philosopher, and by the assistance of Pythagorean societies, it was saved from the orthodox dumbhead, who searched for it, but by more chance than design. For some time it remained in the possession of a German Brotherhood, which we must regard as the last remains of the old Essene Wisdom.

Under this period, the German translation of the Latin original was made public.

Concerning the ancient discovered document, it consisted of a letter from a socalled Theraphute "that is an elder" and in the highest degree of order standing fore-arm for the secret sciences, and the noble purposes which was the aim of the Essene Society.

20

A few years after the crucifixion of Jesus, this person wrote to another elder of the Essene Brotherhood of Alexandria, to inform the Order in Egypt, concerning the rumor about the life and death of Jesus which had come to Alexandria. The miraculous stories which the Disciples of Jesus in their eagerness spread, and which were magnified through the belief of the Jewish peoples in miracles, had in the Essene Order in Alexandria caused much doubt, because the high members of this secret Brotherhood possessed great insight into the powers of nature, and in a natural way sought to explain the supernatural. The rumor about the life of Jesus and his behavior soon convinced the Essenes in Alexandria that Jesus himself must be a member of their Order, so rich in secrets and science, because he used their orders, customs and recognition signs, and because of these facts, they could not accept the rumors about the miracles, because all supernatural explanation of visible phenomena was foreign to the Order. To receive assurance of these facts, an Essene Elder of Alexandria had written to an Elder in Jerusalem, the statement contained in this discovered parchment, and this discovered letter is a complete answer to the questions of the Order in Alexandria. But that an Essene always spoke and wrote the strictest truth is assured because of the known rules of the Essene Order, which places the contents of this old discovered letter beyond doubt. The

Essene Order was strictly virtuous, and was not originated among the Jews, although they existed even
among the Maccabees, and was a still older institution of Pythagorean teaching, which among the
Jewish people had assumed a national outer force.
All members pursued agriculture according to the
rules, sometimes all came together, at others only
those of the higher Degrees. They praised and practiced wisdom and virtue in their religious customs
and speech; they pursued, led by their research in
nature, specially the science of healing; they knew
many effects of minerals and vegetables upon the
human organism, and considered this knowledge a
secret within the higher degrees of their Order, and
used them to relieve the sufferings, physical and
psychical, of the people. Within their Society they
had accepted mutuality in possession and each one
labored for the common treasury. They spoke not
before sunrise upon earthly matters. They held prayers in the beginning of the day. They went in a special suit to labor in the fields. They assembled for a
common meal in mid-day, but dressed, at this time
after they had washed in cold water, in clean, white
linen clothes. In their labor they could not bear servants, so likewise there were no serving brothers,
and they never permitted an uninitiated person to
take part in their meetings. According to their
insight into the secrets of the Order, and also after
their moral worth were they separated into four

degrees. In the lowest or first degree they received mostly children, because the Essenes very seldom married, but if one full grown wished to be received, he must go under a strict moral three years probation before he was received. The highest degree were not permitted to communicate any of their secrets to a lower degree, on penalty of being excluded from the Order. Only a blameless life, virtuous birth and wisdom could gain admission to the highest degrees. They occupied themselves in their daily lives aside from agriculture in edifying and learned conversation, confined strictly to the rules of the Order; practiced charity, and hospitality; they held themselves separate from politics and revolutions, and sought always to establish peace. Their recognition sign and greeting was, "Peace be with you," and with the meal they broke bread and passed the cup. They worshipped Jehovah, but never sacrificed to him in the temple, but worshipped God according to the customs of the Order. They knew no higher virtue than to suffer and die for virtue; death had for them no terrors, because they held the soul as a prisoner in the body to be set free at death, striving upward to the heavenly fields. Untruths and oaths were to them criminal actions, as were quarreling and revenge. Their greatest trust was the sequence of their belief in God and the spirits directly influencing the faith of the people. This Order, which in present Free-Masonry has left its last echo, was in the time of Jesus largely spread over Palestine, as well as in Egypt; and had some colonies and scattered settlements where they came together. They maintained an intimate connection in all societies, and held the Brotherhood near and far always informed in the affairs of the brothers. They are strictly separate from the Oriental fanaticism. In that, they stood high above their contemporaries in culture. There belonged to this Order not only poor, or middle class, and such as had withdrawn from public life, but also many influential public officials and highly eminent accounted themselves members in secret, and council men as well as scribes, labored in secret for the secrets of the Order. From this living Brotherhood in Jerusalem originated the letter which the following leaves communicate in translation. That here one of the Elders of the Order has described and communicated to a brother of his Order the occurrences of which he had been an eyewitness, without fanaticism or prejudice, but with the love of truth, and with pure conception by one of ripened mind in the secrets of the Order, is without doubt. That such a communication should make pretensions to the character of historical objectivity rather than the fanatically elaborate dictation about subjective facts which has been communicated partly from rumor and partly from tradition. And also if the spectator had been in an agitated condition.

EXPLANATION OF THE THREE TRANSLATORS OF THE SWEDISH MANUSCRIPT INTO ENGLISH

A Word of Explanation

A Swedish copy of the German translation spoken of in the above foreword came into the possession of the Muskeegon T. S., who, realizing the importance of the document, called the attention of others to the same, and it has been the joint work of three others, members, to put it into English, and fully realizing that all translations necessarily partake of somewhat of the personality of the translator, it has been our aim in the present instance to make our copy as literal as possible, even sometimes at the expense of a strictly grammatical construction of sentences. Our MSS have been carefully compared with the original from which it was made and pronounced correct. Trusting that it may prove as interesting and instructive to others as it has been to ourselves, we submit it for the perusal of such of our friends as are seeking for statements of facts, leaving it entirely to its own merits, for acceptance or rejection, as it may appeal to their understanding.

Fraternally,

M. H.

J. B. & L. E. B

F.T.S.

25

The Scriptural Story of the Crucifixion

MATTHEW – CHAPTER XXVII, Vs. 26-66

Then released he Barabbas unto them: and when he had scourged Jesus, he delivered him to be crucified.

Then the soldiers of the governor took Jesus into the common hall, and gathered unto him the whole band of soldiers.

And they stripped him, and put on him a scarlet robe.

And when they had platted a crown of thorns, they put it upon his head, and a reed in his hand: and they bowed the knee before him, and mocked him, saying, Hail, King of the Jews!

And they spit upon him, and took the reed, and smote him on the head.

And after that they had mocked him, they took the robe off from him, and put his own raiment on him, and led him away to crucify him.

And as they came out, they found a man of Cyrene, Simon by name: him they compelled to bear his cross.

And when they were come unto a place called Golgotha, that is to say, a place of a skull.

They gave him vinegar to drink mingled with gall: and when he had tasted thereof, he would not drink.

And they crucified him, and parted his garments, casting lots: that it might be fulfilled which was spoken by the prophet. They parted my garments among them, and upon my vesture did they cast lots.

And sitting down they watched him there;

And set up over his head his accusation written, THIS IS JESUS THE KING OF THE JEWS.

Then were there two thieves crucified with him, one on the right hand, and another on the left.

And they that passed by reviled him, wagging their heads,

And saying, Thou that destroyest the temple, and buildest it in three days, save thyself. If thou be the Son of God, come down from the cross.

Likewise also the chief priests mocking him, with the scribes and elders, said,

He saved others; himself he cannot save. If he be the King of Israel, let him now come down from the cross, and we will believe him.

He trusted in God; let him deliver him now, if he will have him: for he said, I am the Son of God.

The thieves also, which were crucified with him, cast the same in his teeth.

Now from the sixth hour there was darkness over all the land unto the ninth hour.

And about the ninth hour Jesus cried with a loud voice, saying, Eli, Eli, lama sabachthani? that is to say, My God, my God, why hast thou forsaken me?

Some of them that stood there, when they heard that, said, This man calleth for Elias.

And straightway one of them ran, and took a sponge, and filled it with vinegar, and put it on a reed, and gave him to drink.

The rest said, Let be, let us see whether Elias will came to save him.

Jesus, when he had cried again with a loud voice, yielded up the ghost.

And, behold, the veil of the temple was rent in twain from the top to the bottom; and the earth did quake, and the rocks rent;

And the graves were opened; and many bodies of the saints which slept arose,

And came out from the graves after his resurrection, and went into the holy city, and appeared unto many.

Now when the centurion, and they that were with him, watching Jesus, saw the earthquake, and those things that were done, they feared greatly, saying, Truly this was the Son of God.

And many women were there beholding afar off, which followed Jesus from Galilee, ministering unto him;

Among which was Mary Magdalene, and Mary the mother of James and Joses, and the mother of Zebedee's children.

And when the even was come, there came a rich man of Arimathea, named Joseph, who also himself was Jesus' disciple:

He went to Pilate, and begged the body of Jesus. Then Pilate commanded the body to be delivered.

And when Joseph had taken the body, he wrapped it in a clean linen cloth,

And laid it in his own new tomb, which he had hewn out in the rock: and he rolled a great stone to the door of the sepulchre, and departed.

And there was Mary Magdalene, and the other Mary, sitting over against the sepulchre.

Now the next day, that followed the day of the preparation, the chief priests and Pharisees came together unto Pilate,

Saying, Sir, we remember that that deceiver said, while he was yet alive, After three days I will rise again.

Command therefore that the sepulchre be made sure

until the third day, lest his disciples come by night, and steal him away, and say unto the people, He is risen from the dead: so the last error shall be worse than the first.

Pilate said unto them, Ye have a watch: go your way, make it as sure as ye can.

So they went, and made the sepulchre sure, sealing the stone, and setting a watch.

MATTHEW-CHAPTER XXVIII, vs. 1-15.

In the end of the sabbath, as it began to dawn toward the first day of the week, came Mary Magdalene and the other Mary to see the sepulchre.

And, behold, there was a great earthquake: for the angel of the Lord descended from heaven, and came and rolled back the stone from the door, and sat upon it.

His countenance was like lightning, and his raiment white as snow:

And for fear of him the keepers did shake, and became as dead men.

And the angel answered and said unto the women, Fear not ye: for I know that ye seek Jesus, which was crucified.

He is not here: for he is risen, as he said. Come, see the place where the Lord lay.

And go quickly, and tell his disciples that he is risen from the dead; and, behold, he goeth before you into Galilee; there shall ye see him: lo, I have told you.

And they departed quickly from the sepulchre with fear and great joy; and did run to bring his disciples word.

And as they went to tell his disciples, behold, Jesus met them, saying, All hail. And they came and held him by the feet, and worshipped him.

29

Then said Jesus unto them, Be not afraid: go tell my brethren that they go into Galilee, and there shall they see me.

Now when they were going, behold, some of the watch came into the city, and shewed unto the chief priests all the things that were done.

And when they were assembled with the elders, and had taken counsel, they gave large money unto the soldiers,

Saying, Say ye, His disciples came by night, and stole him away while we slept.

And if this come to the governor's ears, we will persuade him, and secure you.

So they took the money, and did as they were taught: and this saying is commonly reported among the Jews until this day.

MARK-CHAPTER XV, Vs. 1-11.

And straightway in the morning the chief priests held a consultation with the elders and scribes and the whole council, and bound Jesus, and carried him away, and delivered him to Pilate.

And Pilate asked him, Art thou the King of the Jews? And he answering said unto him, Thou sayest it.

And the chief priests accused him of many things: but he answered nothing.

And Pilate asked him again, saying, Answerest thou nothing? behold how many things they witness against thee.

But Jesus yet answered nothing; so that Pilate marvelled.

Now at that feast he released unto them one prisoner, whomsoever they desired.

And there was one named Barabbas, which lay bound with them that had made insurrection with him, who had committed murder in the insurrection.

And the multitude crying aloud began to desire him to do as he had ever done unto them.

But Pilate answered them, saying, Will ye that I release unto you the King of the Jews?

For he knew that the chief priests had delivered him for envy.

But the chief priests moved the people, that he should rather release Barabbas unto them.

St. JOHN-CHAPTER XIX.

Then Pilate therefore took Jesus, and scourged him.

And the soldiers platted a crown of thorns, and put it on his head, and they put on him a purple robe,

And said, Hail, King of the Jews! and they smote him with their hands.

Pilate therefore went forth again, and saith unto them, Behold, I bring him forth to you, that ye may know that I find no fault in him.

Then came Jesus forth, wearing the crown of thorns, and the purple robe. And Pilate saith unto them, Behold the man!

When the chief priests therefore and officers saw him, they cried out, saying, Crucify him, crucify him. Pilate saith unto them, Take ye him, and crucify him: for I find no fault in him.

The Jews answered him, We have a law, and by our law he ought to die, because he made himself the Son of God.

When Pilate therefore heard that saying, he was the more afraid;

And went again into the judgment hall, and saith unto Jesus, Whence art thou? But Jesus gave him no answer.

Then saith Pilate unto him, Speakest thou not unto me? knowest thou not that I have power to crucify thee, and have power to release thee?

Jesus answered, Thou couldest have no power at all against me, except it were given thee from above: therefore he that delivered me unto thee hath the greater sin.

And from thenceforth Pilate sought to release him: but the Jews cried out, saying, If thou let this man go, thou art not Caesar's friend: whosoever maketh himself a king speaketh against Caesar.

When Pilate therefore heard that saying, he brought Jesus forth, and sat down in the judgment seat in a place that is called the Pavement, but in the Hebrew, Gabbatha.

And it was the preparation of the passover, and about the sixth hour: and he saith unto the Jews, Behold your King!

But they cried out, Away with him, away with him, crucify him. Pilate saith unto them, Shall I crucify your King? The chief priests answered, We have no king but Caesar.

Then delivered he him therefore unto them to be crucified. And they took Jesus, and led him away.

And he bearing his cross went forth into a place called the place of a skull, which is called in the Hebrew Golgotha:

Where they crucified him, and two others with him, on either side one, and Jesus in the midst.

And Pilate wrote a title, and put it on the cross. And the writing was, JESUS OF NAZARETH THE KING OF

THE JEWS.

This title then read many of the Jews: for the place where Jesus was crucified was nigh to the city: and it was written in Hebrew, and Greek, and Latin.

Then said the chief priests of the Jews to Pilate, Write not, The King of the Jews: but that he said, I am King of the Jews

Pilate answered, What I have written I have written.

Then the soldiers, when they had crucified Jesus, took his garments, and made four parts, to every soldier a part; and also his coat; now the coat was without seam, woven from the top throughout.

They said therefore among themselves, Let us not rend it, but cast lots for it, whose it shall be: that the scripture might be fulfilled, which saith, They parted my raiment among them, and for my vesture they did cast lots. These things therefore the soldiers did.

Now there stood by the cross of Jesus his mother, and his mother's sister, Mary the wife of Cleophas, and Mary Magdalene.

When Jesus therefore saw his mother, and the disciple standing by, whom he loved, he saith unto his mother, Woman, behold thy son!

Then saith he to the disciple, Behold thy mother! And from that hour that disciple took her unto his own home.

After this, Jesus knowing that all things were now accomplished, that the scripture might be fulfilled, saith, I thirst.

Now there was set a vessel full of vinegar: and they filled a sponge with vinegar, and put it upon hyssop, and put it to his mouth.

When Jesus therefore had received the vinegar, he

said, It is finished: and he bowed his head, and gave up the ghost.

The Jews therefore, because it was the preparation, that the bodies should not remain upon the cross on the sabbath day, (for that sabbath day was an high day,) besought Pilate that their legs might be broken, and that they might be taken away.

Then came the soldiers, and brake the legs of the first, and of the other which was crucified with him.

But when they came to Jesus, and saw that he was dead already, they brake not his legs:

But one of the soldiers with a spear pierced his side, and forthwith came there out blood and water.

And he that saw it bare record, and his record is true: and he knoweth that he saith true, that ye might believe.

For these things were done, that the scripture should be fulfilled, A bone of him shall not be broken.

And again another scripture saith, They shall look on him whom they pierced.

And after this Joseph of Arimathea, being a disciple of Jesus, but secretly for fear of the Jews, besought Pilate that he might take away the body of Jesus: and Pilate gave him leave. He came therefore, and took the body of Jesus.

And there came also Nicodemus, which at the first came to Jesus by night, and brought a mixture of myrrh and aloes, about an hundred pound weight.

Then they took the body of Jesus, and wound it in linen clothes with the spices, as the manner of the Jews is to bury.

Now in the place where he was crucified there was a

garden; and in the garden a new sepulchre, wherein was never man yet laid.

There laid they Jesus therefore because of the Jews' preparation day; for the sepulchre was nigh at hand.

ST. JOHN-CHAPTER XX.

The first day of the week cometh Mary Magdalene early, when it was yet dark, unto the sepulchre, and seeth the stone taken away from the sepulchre.

Then she runneth, and cometh to Simon Peter, and to the other disciple, whom Jesus loved, and saith unto them, They have taken away the Lord out of the sepulchre, and we know not where they have laid him.

Peter therefore went forth, and that other disciple, and came to the sepulchre.

So they ran both together: and the other disciple did outrun Peter, and came first to the sepulchre.

And he stooping down, and looking in, saw the linen clothes lying; yet went he not in.

Then cometh Simon Peter following him, and went into the sepulchre, and seeth the linen clothes lie,

And the napkin, that was about his head, not lying with the linen clothes, but wrapped together in a place by itself.

Then went in also that other disciple, which came first to the sepulchre, and he saw, and believed.

For as yet they knew not the scripture, that he must rise again from the dead.

Then the disciples went away again unto their own home.

But Mary stood without at the sepulchre weeping: and as she wept, she stooped down, and looked into the sepulchre.

And seeth two angels in white sitting, the one at the head, and the other at the feet, where the body of Jesus had lain.

And they say unto her, Woman, why weepest thou? She saith unto them, Because they have taken away my Lord, and I know not where they have laid him.

And when she had thus said, she turned herself back, and saw Jesus standing, and knew not that it was Jesus.

Jesus saith unto her, Woman, why weepest thou? whom seekest thou? She, supposing him to be the gardener, said unto him, Sir, if thou have borne him hence, tell me where thou hast laid him, and I will take him away.

Jesus saith unto her, Mary. She turned herself, and saith unto him, Rabboni; which is to say, Master.

Jesus saith unto her, Touch me not; for I am not yet ascended to my Father: but go to my brethren, and say unto them, I ascend unto my Father, and your Father; and to my God, and your God.

Mary Magdalene came and told the disciples that she had seen the Lord, and that he had spoken these things unto her.

Then the same day at evening, being the first day of the week, when the doors were shut where the disciples were assembled for fear of the Jews, came Jesus and stood in the midst, and saith unto them, Peace be unto you.

And when he had so said, he shewed unto them his hands and his side. Then were the disciples glad, when they saw the Lord.

Then said Jesus to them again, Peace be unto you: as my Father hath sent me, even so I send you.

And when he had said this, he breathed on them, and saith unto them, Receive ye the Holy Ghost:

Whose soever sins ye remit, they are remitted unto them; and whose soever sins ye retain, they are retained.

But Thomas, one of the twelve, called Didymus, was not with them when Jesus came.

The other disciples therefore said unto him, We have seen the Lord. But he said unto them, Except I shall see in his hands the print of the nails, and put my finger into the print of the nails, and thrust my hand into his side, I will not believe.

And after eight days again his disciples were within, and Thomas with them: then came Jesus, the doors being shut, and stood in the midst, and said, Peace be unto you.

Then saith he to Thomas, Reach hither thy finger, and behold my hands; and reach hither thy hand, and thrust it into my side: and be not faithless, but believing.

And Thomas answered and said unto him, My Lord and my God.

Jesus saith unto him, Thomas, because thou hast seen me, thou hast believed: blessed are they that have not seen, and yet have believed.

And many other signs truly did Jesus in the presence of his disciples, which are not written in this book:

But these are written, that ye might believe that Jesus is the Christ, the Son of God; and that believing ye might have life through his name.

ST JOHN-CHAPTER XXI, Vs. 1-14.

After these things Jesus showed himself again to the disciples at the sea of Tiberias; and on this wise shewed he himself.

There were together Simon Peter, and Thomas called

Didymus, and Nathanael of Cana in Galilee, and the sons of Zebedee, and two other of his disciples.

Simon Peter saith unto them, I go a fishing. They say unto him, We also go with thee. They went forth, and entered into a ship immediately; and that night they caught nothing.

But when the morning was now come, Jesus stood on the shore: but the disciples knew not that it was Jesus.

Then Jesus saith unto them, Children, have ye any meat? They answered him, No.

And he said unto them, Cast the net on the right side of the ship, and ye shall find. They cast therefore, and now they were not able to draw it for the multitude of fishes.

Therefore that disciple whom Jesus loved saith unto Peter, it is the Lord. Now when Simon Peter heard that it was the Lord, he girt his fisher's coat unto him, (for he was naked,) and did cast himself into the sea.

And the other disciples came in a little ship; (for they were not far from land, but as it were two hundred cubits,) dragging the net with fishes.

As soon as they were come to land, they saw a fire of coals there, and fish laid thereon, and bread.

Jesus saith unto them, Bring of the fish which ye have now caught.

Simon Peter went up, and drew the net to land full of great fishes, an hundred and fifty and three: and for all there were so many, yet was not the net broken.

Jesus saith unto them, Come and dine. And none of the disciples durst ask him, Who art thou? knowing that it was the Lord.

Jesus then cometh, and taketh bread, and giveth

them, and fish likewise.

This is now the third time that Jesus shewed himself to his disciples, after that he was risen from the dead.

ST. JOHN-CHAPTER XIX, Vs. 31, 32, 33, 34.

THE JEWS THEREFORE, BECAUSE IT WAS THE PREPARATION, THAT THE BODIES SHOULD NOT REMAIN UPON THE CROSS ON THE SABBATH DAY, (FOR THAT SABBATH DAY WAS AN HIGH DAY,) BESOUGHT PILATE THAT THEIR LEGS MIGHT BE BROKEN, AND THAT THEY MIGHT BE TAKEN AWAY.

THEN CAME THE SOLDIERS, AND BRAKE THE LEGS OF THE FIRST, AND OF THE OTHER WHICH WAS CRUCIFIED WITH HIM.

BUT WHEN THEY CAME TO JESUS, AND SAW THAT HE WAS DEAD ALREADY, THEY BRAKE NOT HIS LEGS:

BUT ONE OF THE SOLDIERS WITH A SPEAR PIERCED HIS SIDE, AND FORTHWITH CAME THERE OUT BLOOD AND WATER.

Letter of the Essene Elder

(From one of the Essene Elders in Jerusalem to one of the Elder Essenes in Alexandria.)

PEACE be with you, dear brethren! You have heard of the things that have happened in Jerusalem and Palestine in general. You were right to believe Jesus to be our brother and a member of our order, of whom his friends among the Romans and the Jewish people relate, that he taught and wrought great wonders, and finally suffered the death of martyrs in Jerusalem. He was born in Nazareth, by the entrance to the beautiful valley into which the river "Kidron" rushes down the steep declivities of the Mount Tabor. He was put under the protection of the order by a member of our brotherhood, by whom his father and mother found a refuge on their flight to Egypt. There are, as you know, many of our brethren living on the borders of Egypt.

In fine, Jesus was admitted into the order contemporaneous with John in their years of early manhood. He lived then in Galilee and had just returned from a visit to Jerusalem, where he was watched by our brotherhood. His initiation took place at Jutha, close by the grand castle of Masseda, where the mountains raise their lofty peaks above the surrounding country. My dear brethren, you may all have been convinced that he has been a member of our order, as well by the doctrines he has taught the people, and his signs of recognition, especially the baptism and the breaking of the bread and passing of the wine, as well as by his being baptized by one of our brethren, John, in Jordan, near the shore of the Dead Sea, in a westerly direction ~ for baptism has, since time immemorial, been a sacred institution in our order. You wonder that the belief in the supernatural and miracles should gain foothold in our midst, when you know that we all have to bear the responsibility for the actions of one of our members.

Therefore, you ought to know that the rumor is like a wind. Where it commences it drives the pure air away ahead, but in its progress it receives all vapors and mist from the earth, and when it has passed some distance it creates darkness instead of the clear pure air, of which it was first composed, and at last consists solely of the particles it has received during its progress. It is even so as regards the rumor about Jesus and his fate.

Furthermore, consider that the inspired men that have written and informed of him, were often carried away by their enthusiasm, and in their devotion and simplicity they believed all the things, the people, naturally superstitious, told about him.

Furthermore, consider that all the secrets of our holy brotherhood at all times remained unknown to the writers, in accordance with our rules, and that only the higher members had any knowledge about the secret assistance and protection Jesus received from us.

Take at last into consideration, that our rigid laws prohibited us from interfering or taking any active part in politics, or infringing upon the counsel or plans of the rulers of the land.

Therefore we have acted quietly and secretly, and have suffered the law to take its course; at the same time we secretly aided and assisted our friend.

Know then that Jesus is our "brother," and has himself vowed, when he at Jutha was admitted in the first degree of our order, that our brotherhood thenceforth should be to him as father and mother, and truly we have proved us as such in accordance with the regulations of our law.

I write this to you, my brethren, in the truth and knowledge of our brotherhood, that you may learn and conceive the truth of what has happened. I inform you of what I know about it, and I have been an eye-witness to all, and secretly taken great interest and active part in all these transactions.

Now that I write this to you, the Jews have seven times ate the lamb of passover since our brother was crucified, whom we all loved and in whom God was glorified. Still I have forgotten none of the incidents that I have lived to see pass, indeed as true as the words are that pass over my lips, and the thoughts that I write, as verily do I believe from the depths of my soul, that Jesus was chosen by God and begotten by the eternal spirit. He called himself the son of God, and he proved himself to be such by teaching in the name of God; lived a holy life, and was well versed in the secrets of nature, human, animal and vegetable. In all these things we acknowledge God; and the man that can say: "Behold, I am of God," verily is so; for he that is not, cannot say it, he not having the word in his heart, and has not learned it from the Spirit.

I will now proceed to relate the parentage of this man, who loved all men, and for whom we feel the highest esteem, that you may have full knowledge of him. He was from his infancy brought up for our brotherhood; indeed he was predicted by an Essene, whom the woman thought to be an angel. This woman was of a very imaginative disposition, prying into the supernatural and mysteries of life, and found great pleasure in everything that she could not explain rationally. Our brother, the Essene, has acknowledged his share in the affair, and compensated by getting the brotherhood secretly to search for and protect the child. And Joseph, who was a man of great experience in life, and great devotion to the immortal truth, was, through a messenger from our order, influenced and advised not to leave the woman, nor to shake her belief in the sacredness of the matter, and to be a father to the child till our brotherhood could admit him as a novice.

Thus, during the flight to Egypt, Joseph was secretly protected and guided by our order, and conducted as a guest to the congregated brotherhood by the Mount "Cassius," at the slope of the mount, on which the Romans have built a temple dedicated to Jupiter. The Essenes who lived there were commissioned to introduce Joseph, his wife and the child into their congregation, that they might see our way of worshipping and praising God, "the creator of all," and learning the ceremony of eating the consecrated bread and drinking the holy wine. At our request they informed our brotherhood in Jerusalem how it all had been executed; that Joseph was placed in the right hand semi-circle among the men, and Mary his wife among the women to the left. There they, with our brethren, ate the bread and drank the wine, and participated in singing the holy hymns. Further, Joseph here vowed before the elder of our memberhood, that he renounced forever any claim on the child, who was thenceforth to belong to the order. He was then made acquainted with the salutation and sign of the holy brotherhood which enabled him during his travels to make himself known to these; they also directed him which route to take to arrive in safety.

This route went through a part of the country where there lived many enlightened, learned Jews, well versed in the scriptures, and devoted to study. Among these our order had many members, who were ordered to protect Joseph and be hospitable to him, even before he arrived. This was in the beautiful country of Heliopolis with its fine forests and hard by the temple of "Jehovah," erected by Onias.

When the peril in Galilee was over and the Roman "Warus" was pillaging in Judea, making the country unsafe, Joseph went to Nazareth, that is situated by the steep mount of "Tabor." But soon Archelaus brought new terror over Galilee, and Joseph was persuaded by our brethren to go to Jerusalem, on his way passing "Luhem," and there seek protection by our brotherhood. This was duly done, and at passover they arrived at "Nisan."

Here I myself spoke with them. I was then in the lower degree of the order, and in obedience to the command of the elder, carried a message to Joseph. He proved to be a candid and experienced man, and spoke with great judgment. Indeed he exhorted Mary to discern distinctly between reality and dreamy imagination, things as different as day and night; and instructed her to quiet her mind through prayer and devotion. It appears that she possessed a very fiery imaginative mind, that often raised her thoughts above earthly matters, and made her indifferent to commonplace things. In consequence she had a good influence in directing the mind of her son to the study of the immortal truths. Far from Joseph blaming her for this, he instructed Jesus in knowledge and wisdom, and protected his pure mind from getting overstrained through his power of imagination.

And when the child Jesus spoke with the scribes about holy things, his doctrines gave great offence to the Pharisees in Jerusalem, as they considered them dangerous and incredible. Because the Pharisees kept strictly to the traditions and details of the Mosaic law, they felt great animosity against everybody who did not exactly believe as they did, and who did not keep the ceremonials of temple service externally. They gave alms conspicuously, taught of "the kingdom of the dead," of the influence of good angels and evil ones, and of the future grand eternal destiny of the Jewish people. Although they had a great many partisans among the common people and held a great deal of power and influence with them, still the Spirit of God did not dwell neither in their houses nor on their tongues.

But Joseph had adopted our doctrines, and without any figurative mysteries he clearly had fixed them in the mind of the growing child. Indeed, the child already then felt for the miseries of the people; and they were raptured to hear him teach the word of God. The scribes knew him to be a Galilean, and they despised him as they despised the whole Galilean people. But some of our brethren went to the temple, and without making themselves known through the holy salutation, kept him in their midst, that they might protect him.

When the divine child had spoken publicly, in the temple, were our brothers apprehensive of danger threatening him, as they discovered the Pharisees and Rabbis to hold a private council how they might banish him from Galilee for the sake of his doctrines. They therefore allured him to the synagogue of Sopherim by taking an assumed interest about the law, as they perceived that in his ardor and enthusiasm for the conversation he heeded nothing else.

Thus it came to pass that he was lost from his father and mother in the large city, that then contained great many people, from the whole country, on account of the passover. Our friends, the Essenes, were informed of this, and did not consider the situation of the child among the Pharisees a safe one, as much more as a Rabbi, who had become a true friend and teacher to the child, no more could be present to moderate his zeal and ardor, contending as he was with the immoral hypocrites, as the Rabbi had gone on a journey to Jericho.

Therefore we informed Joseph and his wife, whom we found in double grief as they at the time also had been informed that the husband of Elizabeth, Mary's friend, had died. Thus she had been searching for her son in three days, in great sorrow, at the same time she felt a great desire to go to see her friend. At last she found him the fourth day at "Sopherim," according to the information given by our brethren.

And Nabbin, the Rabbi who had taken so much

interest in the child, was a secret member of our order, and received orders to protect him.

Thus it came to pass that Mary, her husband and son went back to Jutha.

Here she found her friend Elizabeth in great grief with her son, whose name was "John."

Here the two youths were much together, and talking about the sacred and divine; wandering oft into the wildest parts of the mountains. They grew to be devoted friends, and their attachment grew into intimate acquaintance with each other, in searching for truth. John, Zacharias' son, had already received the doctrine of the Nazarenes, as regards reservedness, and he knew the scriptures and traditions perfectly, but did not comprehend the beautiful and elevated in this world, nor the laws of nature, as well as Jesus. He felt great dislike to the customs of the heathens, and despised and hated tyrants.

And the time had come that Jesus should be admitted into the first degree of our secret order. And in the valley our order had a brotherhood, situated not far from the mountain, where the castle Masseda is erected; and the elder of our brotherhood met them there, and listened to their conversation. He taught that wisdom and virtue were strengthened by fraternity, whereupon Jesus asked to be allowed to take measures for admittance into the order, in enthusiastic transport. The example set by him was followed by John, and the elder offered up a prayer that made Jesus a devotee of God.

According to the rules of the order, the elder now said: "You shall be my brethren as soon as you, by the next new moon, see the glare of fire on the mountain, where the temple is built, where you then will appear. He that is initiated into the order has at the same time devoted his life to serve others. Tell your father Joseph that the time has now come for him to fulfill the vow he made at "mount Cassius."

The Essene then departed. But when the child had got home, Joseph was remembered of his vow and his duties to our brethren. Joseph then made known to Jesus that he was not his father. They kept secret the admission of Jesus into the brotherhood, for fear of the Gaulanites. By the agreed time, in the evening, they saw the signal of fire ascend from the mountain, when they immediately set out for that place, where they were met by the white-robed messengers sent by the brotherhood.

Jesus was initiated according to the rules, as follows: They were both shown the way to enter the assemblage, where the brethren were seated in four separate groups, according to the four degrees. Over the scene the crescent shed its lurid glare. The two were then placed before them, and made the vow, the brethren in their white robes placing the right hand on their breasts, and the left one hanging down by their sides; because none but the pure of heart shall see the holy and sacred. And they vowed indifference to the treasures of this world, worldly power or name, and vowed obedience and secrecy through the brotherly kiss. And, as is our custom, after making the vow these two were conducted into the lonely cavern there for three days and nights for self-trial. In the evening of the third day they were brought back to the assembled brethren to answer the questions put to them, and then pray. Having received the brotherly kiss, they were dressed in the white robes, denoting the sacred purity, and a trowel put in their hands, denoting the task of our brotherhood. Having sung the hymns and partaken of the feast of love by themselves, according to the custom of the order, none of the brethren participating, they were dismissed, and instructed about the trials they were to go through, living alone separate from society for a year, somewhere not too far from the elder of the order, to receive instructions from him, fitting them for the higher degree of our order.

And both of them grew rapidly in divine knowledge. Jesus had a frank, hearty disposition, but John shrouded himself in stern seriousness, and sought solitude. The year having passed, they were again by new moon admitted into the order as real members, and initiated into the higher science. Having given a full account of their doings in the past year, and acted in obedience to all the rules, and performed the ceremonies of praying, singing, and partaking of the feast of love, and conducted to the secret chamber of worship, they were instructed to search in the scriptures.

As the rules of our order permit the admitted member either to remain with the brotherhood or go out into the world either to teach or heal, according to his own wishes, so Jesus chose to go forth teaching, while John wished to execute the duty of a "terapeut," or elder. Jesus felt himself called by the spirit of God, and longed to preach the Essene doctrine to the people.

Thus it came to pass that John returned to Jutha,

to live in solitude in the wilderness, and Jesus went to Nazareth.

Here he proved gloriously his virtue, and fulfilled the vow he had made to the order. His friend "Lazarus" had a sister "Mary," who loved him, and he, in his heart, returned her love.

But, according to the rules, an Essene is not allowed to take unto him a wife, after his own desire that the sacred work shall not thereby be retarded. And Jesus overcame his love for this woman by his dutiful devotion to sacrifice every feeling of selfishness to serve the brotherhood. Still the struggle was hard, and both wept bitterly when they parted.

I have informed you of all this, dear brethren, that you shall indeed know that he was our brother, and belonged to our holy order.

Thus all doubts on this matter must be ended. Jesus, our brother, willingly met death to glorify the doctrine of our order, and the greatest reward for our virtue is to be allowed to sacrifice ourselves for it.

You have heard the information the Jews and his disciples have given about him; that they have seen him in the mountains and on the road after they believed him dead. The divine providence has given us a minute knowledge of these events that is hidden from the people, and we inform you of it in reply to your question on the matter.

Even as I write this, the tears gush from my eyes, and it seems to me I see our brother in his torture and anguish of death; and my afflicted mind is anew wounded by the recollection of his courage and self-sacrifice. He was sent by God, chosen by the Almighty, loved by us all, and inspired both in teaching and the knowledge of nature and its elements.

Hear then, my brethren, what happened in Jerusalem seven passovers ago. I have seen it all with my own eyes, and with my mouth I have kept it a secret, that not the world in general should know it; for the Jews and the heathens do not believe in anything but what they have seen with their eyes, so they have no faith in God, above what they can conceive with their senses. Therefore, my dear brethren, you should give God praise, that it has come to pass thus. We have kept these things a secret, and not let the people know them, lest the belief in providence should be diminished. For you know there are many pious and excellent men who have recorded and remembered the life and death of Jesus, but have them only from rumors, augmented and corrupted by superstition; and very naturally they, from reverence and piety, believe what they hear about a beloved master.

It was even so with them, chosen among the people, who were called Jesus' disciples. Most of them have heard of it only through tradition, as it is told from man to man; although there were others that were present, but these have given no information relating to these important events.

Now I will in secrecy inform you what I and our brotherhood in Jerusalem have seen and been witness to; and you know an Essene never lets anything pass his lips but the strictest truth. Every man that has got the gift of speech ought to glory in God, and give manifestation of him, even as God has given unto him the tongue in his mouth. We might indeed have saved our beloved brother from the vengeance of his enemies, if everything had not come to pass so quickly, and our laws had not forbid us to interfere in public matters.

Still we have saved him secretly, as he fulfilled his divine mission, in the sight of all the universe. Indeed, the fact that a man actually dies for his faith does not increase the glory of God; but that he, full of devotion and divine confidence, will suffer himself to be subjected to the martyrdom for his faith, and this resolution, firmly fixed in a man's mind, constitutes the fulfillment of our work in this world.

Therefore, pay good heed to what I now inform you, that you may judge for yourselves of the rumors that have reached you hence and from Rome.

* * * * * *

(Here is a large vacant place in the document, caused by the destroying influence of time, the deciphering of which is not possible from the still existing remains.)

* * * * * *

The procession in which were the doomed Jesus and the two thieves, wound its way out of the entrance to the valley that leads from Jerusalem to Golgotha to the place of execution. The women cried loudly when they beheld Jesus almost sinking down under the weight of the cross, and his wounds from the scourging that he had undergone, bleeding profusely.

Having arrived at the barren mountain ridge "Gileon," where nothing grows, and which lays on the north side, through which the lonely valley of death winds its way, they halted, and Jesus fell to the ground, his tortured body losing all its strength.

Meanwhile the Roman soldiers were selecting places for erecting the crosses. This done, they wanted to prove their sympathy with the sufferers by giving them a drink that made them unconscious according to the custom before crucifixion. This drink was prepared from sour wine mixed with wormwood and called Toska.

But Jesus did not wish to die for his faith and the truth as a drunkard, wherefore he refused to drink of it, having knowledge of the qualities of the mixture from our order, which he knew by testing it.

And the crosses being erected, the time had now come that the punishment was to be inflicted on Jesus. The first ceremony was to tear his clothes off from him. But to do it, it was necessary to take off the soldier's mantle that he wore after the scourging, and put on him his own clothes, which were then tore off his body as the law bids. At the request of the servants of Sanhedrim, Jesus' cross was placed in the middle between the two thieves, thereby denoting that his was the greatest crime. They had even distinguished his cross from the others, for although they commonly were constructed in such a manner that the perpendicular beam did not reach above the cross-beam, his was of a different form, the perpendicular beam reaching far above the cross-beam. They then laid hold of Jesus, and lifting him up, placed him on the short stake that is always put in front of each cross that the body of the criminal may rest there while being tied. They tied the arms as usual with strong cords, and so tightly that all the blood went back to the heart, and breathing was made difficult. In the same manner they tied his feet, and wound half way up his legs strong cords which drove the circulating blood back to the heart. After this they drove through his hands thick iron nails, but none through his feet, for this was not customary. I note this particularly, my dear brethren, as the rumor says that he was nailed through both hands and feet.

Thus the just hung, exposed to untold sufferings, in the heat of the sun, which that day was uncommonly fierce and fatiguing, while the soldiers took possession of his clothes, according to the custom. The cloak they cut in four parts; but the tunic was woven, and could not be torn asunder, wherefore they cast lots for it.

In the afternoon, when the sun had turned, there came lots of people from the city, drawn thither by curiosity; and there were several priests present, gloating over their sinful vengeance. They derided him, bowed down as he was, with grief and pain, and exhorted the people to mock him.

Jesus suffered quietly, directing his gaze to the sky. He heard not the women of his tribe, from Galilee, that were standing some distance off, wringing their hands, and lamenting his, as they thought, untimely death. These sounds of anguish and lamenting were drowned by the noise made by horsemen advancing to the scene, which was the high-priest "Caiaphas" with a large escort of servants, who came to mock and deride the crucified son of God. And even one of the thieves crucified joined with them in railing him, as he had secretly hoped that Jesus would have delivered both himself and them through a miracle.

Now the Romans had, in derision to the Jews, fixed a plate on the cross, over his head, in four different languages, calling him the King of the Jews. This made the priests angry; but as they feared Pilate, they exhausted their wrath by mocking Jesus.

Darkness descended over the earth, and the people returned to Jerusalem. But Jesus' disciples, his friends and the elders of our holy order remained in Golgotha, our order having close by a colony for worshipping and partaking of our feast of love. And Jesus recognized his mother among the weeping women from Galilee, standing close by the silent John (the evangelist). Jesus called out loudly in the anguish of his pain, citing the twenty-second psalm, praying thereby God to deliver him from his sufferings.

There were still a few Pharisees remaining on the mountain, that intended mocking him, as they had expected and hoped Jesus to descend from the cross, "the worldly saviour of the people"; but as this did not happen, they felt deceived and angry. The heat grew gradually fiercer, more unendurable, and a fire was being prepared in the earth and the air, such as is essential to purifying of the elements. The Essene brethren knew, through their knowledge of nature and its elements, that an earthquake was coming, as had formerly happened in the days of our forefathers.

Towards night the earth was shaking terribly, and the Roman centurion was so terrified that he prayed to his heathen gods. He believed that Jesus was beloved by the gods. Most of the frightened people left the place and returned to Jerusalem; and the

Centurion, who was a noble man of a compassionate character, allowed John to conduct the mother of Jesus close to the cross. Jesus was then very dry, his lips parched, and pain burning in his limbs. A soldier put a sponge dipped in vinegar on a long cane of hyssop, and Jesus quenched his thirst.

As he recommended his mother to the care of John, it was growing darker, although the full moon ought to shine in the sky. From the dead sea was perceived a thick, reddish fog, the mountain ridges round Jerusalem shook violently, and the head of Jesus fell down on his breast. When he uttered his last groan of anguish and pain, and passed away, a whizzing sound was heard in the air; and they of the Jews that still remained were taken by a great fear, as they thought the evil spirits that dwell between heaven and earth were proceeding to punish the people. It was that peculiar sound in the air that precedes an earthquake; and before long the mountain shook, the surrounding country and the city commenced moving, the thick walls of the temple gave way that the vail in the temple parted and fell from its place. Even the rocks cracked, and the hewn sepulchres in the rock were destroyed, as well as many of the corpses kept therein.

And as the Jews thought this very supernatural, so the Roman Centurion believed now in the divinity and innocence of Jesus, and comforted his mother. Although the brethren did not dare to tell the people, as it is a secret with us, they knew very well the cause of this phenomenon of nature, and believed in their brother, without ascribing him any supernatural powers.

Dear brethren, you have reproached us, that we did not save our friend from the cross by secret means. But I only need to tell you the following facts. The sacred law of our order prohibits us from proceeding publicly, and interfering in politics; besides have two of our brethren, influential and experienced, used all their influence with Pilate and the Jewish council in behalf of Jesus, but their efforts were frustrated, by Jesus himself requesting to suffer death for his faith, and to fulfill the law; as you know, to die for truth and virtue is the greatest sacrifice a brother can bring.

There was a certain Joseph, from Arimathea; he was rich, and being a member of the council, he was much esteemed by the people. He was a prudent man, and although he did not seem to belong to any party, he was secretly a member of our sacred order, and lived in accordance with our laws. His friend Nicodemus was a very learned man, and belonged to the highest degree of our order. He knew the secrets of the "Terapeuts," and was often together with us.

Now it happened that after the earthquake, great many people had gone away, when Joseph and Nicodemus arrived at the cross, they were informed of the death of the crucified, in the garden that belonged to our brethren not far from Calvary. Although they loudly lamented his fate, it appeared strange to them that he already was dead, he having hung less than seven hours. They did not believe it, and hastily went up to the place. There they found John alone, he being determined to see what became of the beloved corpse. Joseph and Nicodemus examined the corpse, and greatly moved, the latter pulled Joseph aside and said: "As sure as I know anything about organical life and nature, as sure it is possible to save him." But Joseph did not understand him, and he advised us not to tell John anything of what we had heard. Indeed, it was a secret which was to save our brother from death.

Nicodemus shouted: "We must immediately have the corpse with its bones unbroken, because he may still be saved"; then conceiving his want of caution, he went on in a whisper, "saved from being infamously buried." He persuaded Joseph to set aside his own interests, to save their friend, by immediately going to Pilate, and prevailing upon him to allow them to take Jesus from the cross that very night and put it in the sepulchre, hewn in the rock close by, and which belonged to Joseph.

I understood what he meant, and remained with John to watch the cross, and prevent the soldiers from breaking the bones of Jesus. No corpse is allowed to remain on the cross over night, and the next day being Sunday, they would now take him down and bury him early. The Jewish council had already demanded of Pilate to order the soldiers to break the bones of the crucified, that they might be buried.

Not long after Joseph and Nicodemus had started out, each one on his sacred mission, the messenger arrived and brought order to the Centurion, to take down the corpses and bury them. I was greatly agitated by this information, for I knew he could not be saved, if he was not handled carefully, and still less if his bones were to be broken. Even John was dismayed, though not from fear of the plans being frustrated, that he did not know; but he felt grieved at the thought of seeing his friend maltreated. For John believed that Jesus was dead. As the messenger arrived, I hastened up to him, thinking and hoping that Joseph already might have seen Pilate, but for which there in reality was no possibility.

"Does Pilate send you?" I inquired of him.

And he answered, "I do not come from him but (from) the Secretary who acts for the governor in such unimportant affairs."

The Centurion perceived my anxiety and looked at me, and I said friendly to him: "You have seen that this man that is crucified is an uncommon man, do not maltreat him, for a rich man among the people is now with Pilate to offer him money for the corpse, that he may bury it decently."

My dear brethren, I will here let you know that Pilate often sold the bodies of the crucified to their friends that they might bury them.

And the Centurion was friendly to me as he had conceived from the events that Jesus was an innocent man. When the two thieves were beaten by the soldiers with heavy clubs and their bones broken, the Centurion went by the cross of Jesus, saying to his soldiers: Do not break his bones, for he is dead.

And a man was seen hurrying along on the road from the castle of Antonia to Calvary.

He stepped up to the Centurion and brought the order that he should quickly come to Pilate.

The Centurion then questioned the messenger as to what Pilate wanted of him at this hour of the night. The messenger answered, that he wanted to know if Jesus indeed was dead.

"So he is," said the Centurion, "therefore we have not broken his bones." To be the more sure of it, one of the soldiers struck his spear into the corpse in such a manner that it passed over the hip into the side. The corpse showed no convulsions, and this seemed a sure sign to the Centurion that he actually was dead; and he hurriedly went off to give his report. But from the insignificant wound flowed blood and water, at which John wondered, and my hope revived. For even John knew from the knowledge of our brotherhood that out of a wound in a dead body flows nothing but a little thickened blood; but now flowed thereof water and blood; and I felt very anxious to see Joseph and Nicodemus return.

At last some Galilean women were seen to approach that were returning from Bethania, whither they had brought Mary, Jesus' mother, in care of the "Essene friends." And among the women was Mary, the sister of Lazarus, who had loved Jesus, and she wept loudly. But before she could pour out her grief, for John was gazing intently at the wound in Jesus' side, without paying heed to anything else, Joseph and Nicodemus arrived in a great hurry. Joseph had moved Pilate, through his dignity, and Pilate, having received information about the death of the crucified, gave the body to Joseph, without taking pay therefor.

For Pilate had a great reverence for Joseph, and secretly repented of the execution. When Nicodemus saw the wound, flowing with water and blood, his eyes were animated with new hope, and he spoke encouragingly, forseeing what was to happen. He drew Joseph aside to where I stood, some distance from John, and spoke in a low, hurried tone: "Dear friends, be of good cheer, and go to work. Jesus is not dead; he only seems to be because his strength was exhausted. While Joseph was with Pilate I hurried over to our colony, and fetched the herbs that are useful in such cases. But I advise you not to let John know that we intend to reanimate the corpse of Jesus, for I fear he could not conceal his joy; and dangerous indeed would it be to let the people know it, as our enemies would then put us to death, as well as him."

After this they hurried up to the cross, and, according to the prescriptions of the medical art, they slowly untied his bonds, pulled the spikes out of his hands, and carefully laid him on the ground. Thereupon, Nicodemus spread powerful spices and salves on long pieces of "byssus" that he had brought along, and whose use was only known in our order.

These he wound about Jesus' body, pretending that he done it to keep it from decaying, till after the feast, when he wanted to embalm the body. These spices and salves had a healing influence, and were used by our Essene brethren, who knew the rules of medical science to annihilate the effects of death-like fainting. And even as Joseph and Nicodemus were bending over his face and their tears fell on him, they blew into him their breath, and warmed his temples.

Still Joseph felt doubtful, but Nicodemus encouraged him to increase their efforts. Nicodemus spread balsam in both hands, but he thought it best not to tie up the wound in his side, because he considered the flow of blood and water to be beneficial for the respiration and renewing of life.

In his grief and sorrow John did not at all believe in life returning to his friend, and did not hope to see him again before in "Sheol."

The corpse was then laid in the sepulchre made in the rock, which belonged to Joseph. They smoked the grotto with aloe and other strengthening herbs, and as the corpse was placed on moss, still stiff and inanimate, they placed a large stone in front of the entrance, that the vapors might better fill the grotto.

This done, John, with some others, went to Bethania, to comfort his grief-stricken mother.

But "Caiaphas" had sent out secret spies, although it was Sabbath. He was anxious to learn who were Jesus' secret friends, for he had suspicions on Pilate for having given Joseph of Arimathea the body without any pay, he being rich, a Rabbi and member of the high council, who never had appeared to take any interest in the case of Jesus previously, but now had given his own place of burial for the crucified. And Caiaphas anticipated secret plans between the rich Joseph and the Galileans, and knowing that they intended to embalm the corpse, he hoped there to catch them, as the idea struck him that Joseph and Pilate were plotting against the Jews. This fear caused him a great deal of anxiety, and he tried to conceive some means of secret accusing Joseph and take him a prisoner. Thus he betrayed himself in sending late in the night a number of his armed servants to an obscure valley close by the grotto in which was Jesus' corpse. Some distance from them were stationed a detachment of the temple guard, to assist the servants of the high priest, if necessary. But the rumor has told you the guard were Roman soldiers, which was not the case. The high priest even mistrusted Pilate.

Meanwhile Nicodemus had with me hastened to our brethren, and the oldest and wisest came to confer as to the best means of restoring Jesus to life. And the brethren agreed immediately to send a guard to the grove. Joseph and Nicodemus hurried to the city, there to fulfill their further mission.

And after midnight, towards morning, the earth again commenced shaking, and the air felt very oppressive. The rocks shook and cracked, red flames burst forth from the crevices, illuminating the red mist of morning.

This was a dreadful night. Beasts horrified by the earthquake, went howling and scampering about, the little lamp in the grotto threw through the narrow opening trembling shadows in the horrible night, and the servants of the high priest were full of fear, listening to the whizzing in the air and the roaring in the earth.

One of our brethren went to the grave in obedience to the order of the brotherhood, dressed in the white robe of the fourth degree. He took a secret path, that ran through the mountains to the grave, and only was known to the order.

When the cowardly servants of the high priest perceived the white-robed brother on the mountain, undefined by the morning mist, gradually approaching, they were taken with a great fear and thought that an angel was descending from the mountain. When the brother arrived at the grave which he was to guard, he rested on the stone that he had pulled from the entrance, according to his orders, when the soldiers fled and reported that an angel had driven them away.

When the Essene youth had sat down on the stone came a new shock, and a draft of air passed down the grotto, blew out the lamp, and gave place for the morning light.

Now thirty hours had passed since the assumed death of Jesus. And when the brother heard a slight noise in the grotto, and stepped in to watch what would happen, he smelt a strange odor in the air, as is natural when the earth is going to vomit fire. And the youth saw with untold joy that the corpse moved the lips and breathed. He hastened to assist him, and heard slight sounds rise from his breast, the face assumed a living appearance, and the eyes opened and gazed astonished at the novice of our order.

This happened just as I went off with the brethren of the first degree, from the council, with Joseph, who had called for to consult, how to bring help.

Nicodemus, who was an experienced physician, said on the road, that the peculiar atmosphere prepared in the air by the revolution of the elements, was beneficial to Jesus, and that he never had believed that Jesus actually was dead. And he spoke of, that the blood and water that flowed from the wound was a sure sign that life was not extinct.

Conversing thus, we arrived at the grotto, headed by Joseph and Nicodemus. We were in all twenty-four brethren of the first degree. Entering, we perceived the white-robed novice kneeling down on the moss-strewn floor of the grotto, supporting the head of the revived Jesus on his breast.

And as he recognized his Essene friends, his eyes sparkled with joy, and his cheeks were tinted with a light red; and he sat up, asking: "Where am I?" Then Joseph embraced him, folded him in his arms, told him how it all had come about, and how he was saved from actual death by a profound fainting fit, that the soldiers on Calvary had thought was death. And Jesus wondered, and felt on himself; and praising God, he wept by the breast of Joseph. And Nicodemus urged his friend to take some refreshments, and he ate some dates and some bread dipped in honey. And he gave him some wine to drink, after which Jesus felt greatly refreshed, so he raised himself up. He then became conscious of the wounds in his hands and in his side, but the balsam that Nicodemus had spread on them had a good effect, so they had already commenced to heal.

After the "Byssus" wrappings had been removed and the muckender was taken off his head, Joseph spoke and said: "This is not the place to remain in any longer; the enemies might discover our secret, and betray us." But Jesus was not yet strong enough to walk far, wherefore he was conducted to the house belonging to our order, that lays close to Calvary, in the garden, that also is owned by our brethren.

Another young brother of our order was dispatched to assist the novice that had been watching by the grave of Jesus, to annihilate every trace of the Byssus wrappings and the medicines and drugs used.

When Jesus had arrived unto the brethrens'

house he felt very weak; the wounds began to cause him pain. He was much moved, as he considered all as a miracle. "God has let me rise," said he, "that he may prove in me what I have taught, and I will show my disciples that I do live."

And after a little while the two young men that had been sent to put the grave in order, came hurriedly and brought the message that the friends of Jesus soon would come to seek him.

And they related how they had heard a noise, when occupied in the grotto, as of a great many people coming to the fence that surrounds the garden. When they retired further into the grotto, came a woman on the road from Jerusalem, and showed a great fear by the sight of the stone being rolled away from the grave. She had thought that something had happened to the corpse, and hurried to Bethlehem. But soon after other women came from Jerusalem, and stepped up to the grave. Wondering greatly, they had entered the grave, and one of them in looking for the corpse in the place where it had laid, had seen the brother, and, terrified, pointed him out to her friends. When the other brother also came in view, the women had fallen on their faces, and thought they had seen angels.

And the brethren spoke to them as they had been ordered by them of the first degree, and one of them said to the women: "Jesus is risen. Do not look for him here; say to his disciples that they will find him in Galilee," and the other told them to gather the disciples and conduct them to Galilee.

This was instituted by the wisdom of Joseph, for

he would not that they should look for Jesus at Jerusalem, for his safety's sake. And the brethren stepped out of the cavern by the rear entrance, and noticed that some of the women hastened on the road to Bethania, whereupon the young brethren hurried to us in the house to inform us of what had passed.

Thus the Essene friends tried to persuade Jesus to keep hidden, for his safety's sake, and to recover his strength. But Jesus felt a great desire to prove to his friends that he lived, and of the desire feeling refreshed and strengthened, he asked for clothes, and received immediately the Essene working-garb, such as our brethren wear in their work; dressed in which he appeared as a gardener.

The two young brethren had again gone to the grave, as their work there was not yet completed; and there saw the same woman return who came first to the grave, as John and Peter had meantime made known among the disciples what had happened. And she thought the two novices were angels guarding the empty grave, and she wept.

One of them, of kind disposition, and in a harmonious voice, spoke to the woman, asking her why she wept. This woman was Mary, whom Jesus had loved and had to leave, in accordance with the laws of our holy brotherhood.

And as she was lamenting over that Jesus did not lay where he had been placed before the Sabbath, stood Jesus behind her, dressed in the garb of a gardener.

Animated by the desire to see those he loved again, and to proclaim for them that he lived, he had not taken the advice of the brethren to keep hidden, and leaving the house, had taken the path through the garden to the rock where the grave was hewn.

When Mary saw him she took him to be the gardener; but Jesus knew her, and rejoiced in her love and spoke to her. Still she did not know him, as he looked very weak and suffering; but when he exclaimed, "O Mary!" she knew him, and wanted to kiss his feet, and thereafter embrace him. But Jesus felt the pain in his hands and side, and feared the effects of the hearty embrace, cautiously stepped back a few paces, and said: "Touch me not. Still I live, but I soon shall go to my father in heaven; for my body has become feeble and soon shall be dissolved, that my death may be fulfilled."

As the woman still was knelt down, and with great excitement gazed up to him, Jesus heard the approaching sound of footsteps, and careful for his safety, hastened back, placing himself behind the garden wall, not far from the garden of our friends.

And the two youths who were to guard the grave, and had been instructed to throw the spy enemies from the track of the revived, had seen and heard all this.

Meanwhile Joseph, Nicodemus and the other brethren had stepped from the house into the garden to look after Jesus and take care that he was not in peril on account of his great weakness. This Nicodemus feared having noticed that the wounds were more inflamed and the places where the strong cords had been placed had assumed a dark color. When we arrived at the entrance of the garden, we saw Jesus standing behind the wall, resting against it as if his legs would carry him no more.

It was by this time that John had hastened from the city, looking into the grotto had found this vacant wherefrom the two youths had made their way to our garden, through the secret entrance to the grotto. And also Peter arrived there, and both searched all through the grotto for signs of the corpse, and entering the inner part, they found the muckender in a corner where the novices had thrown it, when they fled at the arrival of the two strange persons. In earnest conversation the two disciples hurried back to the city.

And Jesus had slowly walked along the wall and reached the little gate that opens to the valley by Mount "Gihon," there he listened to the conversation of some women outside the wall. He stepped out and the women believed that they saw an apparition. But he spoke to them to show them that it was himself. And as the youth in the grove having told the women that in Galilee they should see him, one of them remembering this said to him: "Lord shall we obey the word of the angel, and see thee again in Galilee?" Their question astonished Jesus, for he did not know that the brethren had informed the novice to name that part of the country. After considering for a while he answered: "Yes, inform my friends and tell them that I go to Galilee, there you will see me."

His weakness being increased he felt that he ought to be alone; and the women went off. And we his secret protectors went to him and conducted him back to the house that he might rest himself. Nicodemus again tied up his wounds, gave him a medical draught and advised him to keep quiet. But

Jesus feared not death, and was in good spirits. But his strength was exhausted, and he fell into a profound slumber, when Joseph, Nicodemus and the brethren held a council how they might put him in safety. They sent, therefore, some brethren to the city to learn the rumors of Jesus among the people.

And the rumors had told of many miracles in the city, the fleeing guards having tried to conceal their cowardly fear by reporting of terrible events that had taken place, and spirits that had bursted open the grave. And the high-priest had been informed of this, and did not know what to think of it. He feared that the miracle would excite the people; as the people already were busy discussing the miracle, for the women, and even the men, had been too excited thereby to keep it a secret. Therefore, Caiaphas gave the guard money, that they should report that his partisans had stolen the corpse, that they (the disciples) might say he was risen, and thus delude the people.

And Jesus remained all day in his profound slumber, and was filled with new vitality. It was evening before he woke up; his wounds did not now cause him as much pain, as the balsam that Nicodemus had applied had had a good effect. He was in good spirits, and with thankful heart he saw his friend watch over him. He rose from his couch without any assistance, and asked for food, as he felt hungry.

Having refreshed himself, he said: "Now I am strong it behooveth me not to live in concealment. A teacher ought to be with his disciples, and a son embrace his mother."

Joseph answered: "The brotherhood is father and mother to thee, according to their promise, and it is the duty of the brotherhood to protect thee as its beloved child."

And Jesus said: "I do not fear death, for I have fulfilled it, and the enemies shall acknowledge that God has saved me, and will not that I die eternally."

Then one of the elders of the brotherhood said: "Thou art not safe in this country, for they will search after thee. Do not, therefore, go any more among the people to teach, for what thou hast taught will always live among thy friends, and thy disciples will publish it. Remain dead to the world; the brotherhood has brought thee back to life through its secrets, therefore live henceforth for the holy order to which thou belong; live in the privacy of wisdom and virtue, unknown to the world. And we will secretly teach and assist the disciples among the people, and they shall receive encouragement and assistance from the holy brotherhood. And if the time comes that thou shouldst again go out among the people, we will send for thee, and inform thee."

But Jesus, in the ardor of sacred enthusiasm, said: "The voice of God is more powerful in me than is the fear of death. I will see my disciples once more, and go to Galilee."

Then the elder said: "Be it so, as God has called you; but it behooves men to be wise and cautious in good things. Therefore, some of our brethren shall go with thee, and protect thee through our connections in Galilee."

But Nicodemus did not approve of the journey, for

Jesus' body was not as strong as his soul indicated. And the faithful physician represented to him that he would thereby make it impossible to recover his health.

But Jesus answered, "Be it fulfilled that is to be"; and Joseph wondered greatly at the spirit of Jesus, and more than ever believed in his great promises.

When evening had come, Jesus started on his journey, and he wished to go alone. The brethren gave him a warm mantle, it being quite chilly, in which he wrapped himself, that the officers of the city might not recognize him. And the brethren advised him to stop only with the Essene friends, and not travel on the highway, on account of the feast. Therefore Jesus made up his mind to take the road by Bethania and the Ephraimitical mountain, where Samaria bounds on upper Galilee to the north.

And Jesus took his departure, and set out. When he had gone, the brethren blessed his journey, but, advised by Joseph, they sent a novice to follow in his tracks, and on the road secretly inform the Essene friends.

Of all that has happened our friends have inform-ed us.

And while Jesus was on the road to Emaus, a few hours' travel hence, his soul was filled by inspirations over the new life, and he spoke loudly, so that our messenger could hear that it was of the prophecies of Daniel. Two men were traveling the same road from Jerusalem, and they had soon overtaken Jesus, as they walked faster than he.

Jesus said to them, "Peace be with you." He believed he had met Essene friends, but shortly he recognized them as two of his friends of the people, who had often heard him teach. They paid no attention to the quiet traveler. But he heard them speak of his death, and the despair of his disciples. And from their words he conceived that his doctrine was in fear of being annihilated through the lack of hope displayed by his friends, who were in want of a master, to hinder them from becoming separated. And when one of these wanderers lamented that the prophecy had not been fulfilled, and Jesus had not risen from the dead, Jesus spoke with ardor, and the two disciples took a great interest in the conversation of the traveler, as it appeared to them that they had heard the same teachings before.

But where they stopped they retained Jesus, when he wanted to go farther on, all alone in the night. And at the common feast of love in the house, they recognized Jesus; but he did not wish to be known in this place, and secretly passed out through the door, and went to the house of the Essene friend to whom he had been recommended.

Meanwhile, the two disciples retraced their steps to Jerusalem to bring the information of the risen one to their friends there, and found Peter, and with him John.

But the Essene friends held a counsel about what they were further to do. Here was also the youth that our order had sent after him. And Jesus conceived that he immediately must return to Jerusalem to reanimate the hope of his friends and correct the information given by the two disciples, that so hurriedly had returned to Jerusalem. The Essene friend gave him a beast of burden that he might mount and thus travel easier, and the novice, whom we had sent, accompanied him walking by the side of the animal.

And thus it happened that, not long after the arrival of the disciples, Jesus arrived to the well-known home, where our friends used to come together. Jesus gave the sign by which the bar fell from the door by the hand of the doorkeeper, for the disciples were holding a secret counsel. When Jesus heard how his partisans spoke of his resurrection, and were discussing how it were possible, he stepped up among them, and as they at first did not know him, they were alarmed, not knowing that the door had been opened. But he spoke to them, comforted them, and proved to them that he was really flesh and bones. Then they joyfully surrounded him, touched his hands, and Jesus leaned against the breast of John, feeling faint after the fatigues of the travel. Having rested a little he still more proved to his friends that he lived as other people by asking for some food. As the friends had already eaten, there was some bread, honey, and fried fish left, of which he ate and refreshed himself. He exhorted them to fulfill the work and not to give up but be of good cheer, and he blessed them and said that he could not tell them where he went to, that he would go alone, but when they wanted him he would come to them as he yet had a great deal to say to them.

Outside the door the novice was waiting with the animal, and Jesus stepping out demanded to be brought to the quiet dwelling of the Essenes. But another Essene youth had arrived to seek information of him in Jerusalem, and the two now were obliged to carry Jesus between them, as he was very weak and faint, which was occasioned by the fatigue he had undergone on his journey. And after hard work they brought him in the night to the brotherhood, to the house of the elder, that is situated a few stadis from Jerusalem, close by the olive mountain. Here Jesus was placed on a soft bed of moss, where he fell in a profound slumber. And the Essene youths hastened to Joseph, Nicodemus and the other Essene friends to inform them what had happened.

Before the break of day a council was held that they might further protect Jesus, he having ventured back to Jerusalem so openly, for the sake of the holy spirit, that he might strengthen his partisans in their work. And all agreed that no time was to be lost, the priests in the city having their secret spies, who even tried to entrap his disciples. All agreed, that were in the council, that he immediately must depart hence, that he might not be found, and that he ought to return to the quiet valley, not far from Jutha and the castle of Masseda, where there is a wild, mountainous country. Here Jesus had lived before, together with John the physician, and with him admitted to the holy order of our brethren. This was also considered a safe place, as many Essenes lived there.

While they yet were discussing, Jesus awoke from his sweet slumbers, and wondered to see himself surrounded by his brethren. But Joseph and Nicodemus tried to persuade him to save himself, and not again fall into the hands of the priests, and Joseph even told him that he had been informed that Caiaphas had fixed his suspicion on him, that he, with the Galileans, formed a secret plot to overthrow the present state of things, and would demand an explanation why he had laid Jesus in his own grave. He even has suspicion on Pilate for secret combination with me, because he had given the supposed corpse to me without taking pay. And as Joseph persuaded Jesus with much ardor to comply with his wishes, and all the elders supported him, Jesus answered: "Be it so; but I conjure you to encourage my disciples, assist and protect them, and tell them that they shall have no doubts, for I am still with them in body and spirit." And Joseph tried to persuade him to take more rest, as Nicodemus expressed his fear that the excitement and enthusiasm of Jesus would endanger and not be beneficial to his martyred body; for even if the wounds in his hands began to heal, and the wound in his side emitted no more humor, his body was still very weak, and tormented by the excitement of his mind, for having slept, he immediately felt refreshed.

After considering a while, Jesus continued: "If my disciples are not convinced that I really live, and I do not step forth among them, they will think me an apparition and delusion of their imagination."

Joseph answered: "Let us advance John to the higher degrees of our order, that he may be convinced of thy living, and execute thy directions, and inform the other disciples of thee."

But the elders of the brethren objected to John being admitted into all the secrets as he was only in the lowest degree, and they feared he might in his ardor inform others that Jesus was here.

While they yet were discussing, a novice of our order arrived, who had been sent to the city, and he reported that John, with his friends, had hurried to Bethania, to comfort the women in Lazarus' house, and inform them that Jesus had rested, alive, on his bosom. And John had wondered that Jesus had not directed him to go to Galilee, as he had ordered the women, therefore he did not think it was the intention of his master, and that the disciples ought to wait for coming events.

And Jesus remained all day with the Essene friends; and night coming on, we all took the secret road, Joseph, Nicodemus and the elders of the order, and having passed the valley of Rephaim, we reached Masseda at daybreak; and following a narrow path that only was known to the Essenes, we arrived to the brethren in that wild valley.

And the elder provided for Jesus; and when Joseph and we others took our departure, Jesus gave us his word that he would remain there till the father called him to fulfill his mission.

And the brethren sent a messenger every day to us to inform us of the state of health of our highly beloved brother. And we were informed that Jesus had rested for several days, but that his heart was sad and filled with melancholy thought. This was the same valley where he had wandered with John his beloved companion, and with him been initiated into the holy order. And he meditated on that John having as a physician founded a school and baptized, had been slain by the enemies, while he had been saved by the hand of God, wherein he saw the command of God not to rest, as his body must have been restored for some purpose.

This thought excited his mind, as he came to the place where he and John had solemnly vowed to die for truth and virtue, he felt called to pursue the mission in the cause of which his friend had died. And Jesus went every day to the blessed spot, and refreshed his body, viewing the splendor of nature. And he chose a spot, where he could see the high tower of Masseda toward the west, protected from the morning and noon sun by high mountains, while on the other side the view was unobstructed, and the country open toward the sea and the valley of Sittim.

But the elder of the brotherhood did not leave him alone, as he perceived that Jesus often would lie in deep reveries, and his longing to see his disciples would overcome his care for his own safety.

But by this time our brethren of the brotherhood in Jerusalem remembered the promise they had made to Jesus to protect his disciples, and strengthen them in their belief in the resurrection of their master, and had been informed that not all the disciples were convinced of the resurrection of their master. And one of them that doubted was Thomas, who was a great thinker, and had received his education from the Essene brethren. For that reason he possessed great knowledge in the secret powers of nature. He explained the events that had taken place, scientifically, and did not believe in any miracle, for, as all Essenes, he was raised above superstition.

But Thomas viewed Jesus' mission as an event of more than ordinary importance, and Jesus confided in him and told him his mission. This Jesus did on account of that Thomas was a very clear-sighted and rational man, excitement and passion being utterly unknown to him; and before being convinced of any-thing, he would try it with great perseverance.

And as the disciples were together in their secret place of meeting, Thomas argued with them, not believing that a man can rise from the grave. But John had himself felt Jesus on his breast, still he could not convince Thomas, although he expected that the prophecies of the prophets were to be fulfilled.

For, dear brethren, the Jews hoped to see Messias come in the manner Elias had proclaimed.

And as our brotherhood had promised to report all, especially as the disciples themselves disagreed, it was to be feared that their ardor in the good cause would diminish; we therefore sent two youths to the valley at Masseda to inform the brethren that they might counsel with Jesus. But Jesus had hardly received the information when he wanted to leave the solitude, and show himself to his disciples. And as the messengers reported that Thomas would not believe in the life of Jesus, except he could feel his hands and the wound in the side, Jesus could re-strain himself no longer, and even the elder advised him to go there and convince them.

This happened the seventh day that Jesus had been in concealment.

Thus it happened that our brethren accompanied Jesus; and on the eighth day, as the disciples were together in Jerusalem, Jesus stepped forth among them, and convinced Thomas. Having done this, he spoke to his disciples, and he disclosed to them that they were not safe for his sake. He also exhorted to faith and unanimity. But he could not tell time and place where to meet him in Galilee, as he first had to consider thereon.

After this he went away in the evening, accompanied by John. And outside the house there was an Essene youth, who wanted to commit himself to his service; and Jesus sent him away to report that he was in Bethania.

He, thereupon crossed Kidron with John and the night was a beautiful one, and the moon shed a dim light on the scene. At Gethsemane, Jesus rested by the wall and spoke with John about his martyrdom and sufferings, and having received information of his disciples, he sent him on ahead to the house of Lazarus in Bethania, that he might announce the arrival, and find out whether he there would be safe or not.

And immediately after Jesus went into the house to see his mother and his friends. Having thanked God for being allowed to see each other once more, they ate supper together and the whole next day he remained with them comforting them and exhorting them to believe in the truth, and warned them of false expectations, they having come to think that he would forever remain with them.

And he told them that it now was time for him to

go, as night had come. He would hasten to Galilee, to strengthen his disciples to persevere in the good work.

But even while Jesus was in Bethania, dangers were threatening him. Caiaphas the high-priest had been informed that Jesus had been seen in Jerusalem. And he had spread the rumor that disciples had stolen his corpse and invented a miraculous story. But there were many of the people in the city, who believed that Jesus had risen by the hand of God, and they commenced complaining of the injustice done to him, and to believe in the doctrines of Jesus. And the high-priest feared a revolution, and thought that the Galileans intended to overthrow the government, and set up a new ruler, and therefore he was strictly on his watch.

In the evening Nicodemus came to our brotherhood and brought the information that Joseph of Arimathea was arrested, and that they falsely attributed him criminal purposes, as he had been in secret connection with Jesus, whereby a great anxiety rose among the brethren, as we feared that also Jesus had been arrested, as he had not been seen by us since the evening that he convinced Thomas.

Our elders then held a council, when it was agreed that we should search for Jesus, and use all efforts to liberate Joseph.

And two brethren were commissioned to dress themselves in their white holiday-garb, and search for Jesus in Bethania, as Jesus had informed the Essene youth that he would go thither. And as they came to Bethania, in the evening, and in the moon-light saw Lazarus' house at no great distance, they met with a man on the secret road, who carefully scanned the road. But the Essenes recognized him, and asked him if Jesus was at his house. This Lazarus acknowledged, the men having made themselves known, and added that Jesus intended that very night to go to Bethania, and therefore he had examined the road to see if it were safe.

The brethren were conducted into the house, where they spoke with Jesus in a small private room. And when the brethren had told Jesus of the arrest and danger of Joseph, Jesus recommended him to the protection of the order, prayed to God, and thereafter sent John to Jerusalem to warn the disciples of their danger; and having taken leave of the women, we were accompanied by Lazarus as far as Gilgal. Thence he went on further all alone in the night, and early in the morning he found himself by Jordan, in the place where he through John was baptized by the order.

Our holy brotherhood in Jerusalem was now planning how to liberate Joseph, whereto we were in possession of many secret means.

And John had warned his friends, the disciples, as he had been ordered. And the next morning they repaired to the Galilean border in great numbers.

Arriving at the border, they asked of each other: "Whither shall we go ~ our master has fixed no time nor place?" And they thought of their households from which they had been separated for a very long time, and as they were discussing if they should search for Jesus in Nazareth or Capernaum, Peter said: "Let us provide for sustenance, and not be idle, but work till the master calls us to a higher work." After this speech they resolved to take hold of their former trades, and Peter repaired to Bethsaida, where some of the others also arrived in a few days, to assist him and get his counsel. And Peter was a skillful fisherman, and invited the others to go to sea in the evening.

But Jesus made only short day marches, and stopped on the road only with the Essene friends who lived in the valleys. And these brethren were well informed by the brotherhood in Jerusalem of all that had happened to us, and Jesus received of them the information only a few days afterward, that Joseph was liberated from the prison, and on his way to meet him.

And when Jesus declared his intention to step forth in Galilee in places where he had been known before, the Essene friends persuaded him not to do this, and explained to him the danger he was in. And Jesus heeded them, and reflected on where he would meet with his disciples. For that purpose he chose a safe, lonely place, where he was not known, and where there was opportunity for his disciples to dwell.

But the Essene friend had been advised by the elder of the brotherhood in Jerusalem, to choose for a place of meeting the lonely valley at the foot of Mount Carmel, for there live many Essenes, and it was a very fine country. The valleys abound in powerful herbs, and the odor they give is healthy to the wanderer. From that place our brotherhood receives the herbs that the physicians use in medicines. The clear water runs sparkling from the rocks, that contain many caverns, useful to dwell in by they who seek the solitude.

And when the Essene brethren advised Jesus to go to this country, he remembered how the prophets of old were reported to have lived in the same place, Elias, as well as Elisha. He made up his mind to go there, as he there could teach his disciples without fear of his enemies finding out, for this country was inhabited by our brethren only.

But Jesus refused to be accompanied by any of the brethren, and went alone the road to Bethsaida, there to stay with Simon, who was one of his disciples. Arriving at the shore of the Galilean sea in the morning, he found a hut that Peter had built for his convenience in pursuing his trade. And he found Peter, and with him John, fishing. Here Jesus refreshed himself, partaking with them of the feast of love, and was informed that all the disciples had agreed to come together in Bethsaida, to discuss what to do.

But Jesus called them to Mount Carmel, as he had promised the Essenes. And on the evening of the next day Jesus again pursued his journey.

Jesus having rested and refreshed himself for several days at the foot of Mount Carmel, and was prepared to teach, did his disciples arrive, bringing with them several hundred of his partisans; for in this lonely valley they were safe from danger, and the account of Jesus' resurrection had created quite an excitement in Galilee. But many of them had come from mere curiosity, as they wanted to see Jesus do wonders and miracles. Others hoped for the new kingdom of Messias, delivering the Jews from the Romans. But this illustration of his mission grieved Jesus very much, as he had often spoken concerning this, saying that it was absurd to clothe the son of God with worldly power and splendor. And the Essene brethren did not participate in this error, as they well knew that, according to the laws of the order that he had vowed to keep, our brethren can take no part in politics, nor aspire to worldly power.

And the people desiring much to see Jesus, they were informed by the disciples, that the meeting would take place early in the morning. Jesus descended from the summit of the mountain, where the fog assumed a reddish color from the sun, and as he wore the white robe of the Essene order, the people imagined him to be a supernatural being, and throwed themselves down, with their faces to the ground. And many of the people were terrified, and stepped aside out of the road.

And Jesus spoke with a loud voice, saying that he had not come to found a school, but the kingdom of God on earth, through wisdom and virtue. And he instituted baptism, and informed his disciples about the knowledge that he had learned from the elders, how to heal the sick, decide the virtues of minerals and herbs as medicines, make beasts harmless, count- eract poison, etc., etc.

And the disciples and the people that had come with them, remained several days in the valley, and Jesus taught them how to live and preach the doctrine in his name.

But the Essene brethren were informed by the elder of the brotherhood in Jerusalem, that the se- cret messengers of the priests and the grand council had been told of the excitement in Galilee, and that many people repaired to the valley of Mount Carmel. And the brethren warned Jesus of his danger, that he might keep out of his enemies' way, and fulfill his mission, for they were secretly informed, that Cai- aphas intended quietly to arrest and assassinate Jesus, as he believed him to be a deceiver.

And Jesus sent away his hearers and told them, that, if they wanted to speak with him afterwards, they must go to Bethabara, where he would expect them. Having spoken much to the people and teached them, he was fatigued and wanted rest.

And the time came when the Essenes partake of their feast of love. And all the brethren in the valley came together in the house where Jesus dwelled. And Joseph of Arimathea, and Nicodemus and we elders of the brotherhood in Jerusalem departed to be together with him.

But Jesus was weak, and the joy he felt by seeing his beloved friends Joseph and Nicodemus excited him very much. And he spoke much about his death. "Do not misapprehend me if I have not, in everything, lived in compliance with the rules of our brotherhood. For if I had worked in secret, like you, the truth would not been known to the people. Even in public can the wise practice wisdom, the chosen virtue."

And Jesus exhorted all the brethren to lay aside their secrecy and step forth among the people, and to unite with his disciples to teach together with them.

And the words he spoke took root in the hearts of many of the brethren, and therefore I now find many of them witness for Jesus, and have left their solitude.

And Joseph spoke to Jesus: "Knowest thou that the people that does not altogether understand your doctrine, is meditating to proclaim you a worldly king, to overthrow the Romans? But thou must not disturb the kingdom of God through war and revolution. Therefore choose the solitude, live with the Essene friends and be in safety, that your doctrine may be proclaimed by your disciples."

But the elders of the brotherhood were reflecting that it would make a great excitement among the people if Jesus were to disappear like the sun in the evening, and not reappear.

But Jesus feared that the words of Joseph might prove true, and he would not suffer blood to flow for his sake, nor any revolution to cause destruction.

Therefore he consented to go into solitude, his body being very weak. And he went to Bethania, accompanied by Joseph and Nicodemus. On the road they conversed together about the secrets of the brotherhood; and Jesus desired to take leave of his friends in Bethania, and return to the lonely country near the Dead Sea.

In Bethania he comforted his mother, the other friends and Lazarus, and illustrated to them that in his doctrine he always remained with them. But the account of Jesus' being in the vicinity of Jerusalem had soon become known to all his partisans, and many came together and were instructed to repair to a secret place at a fixed time. Thither now Jesus repaired.

And several hundred people had come together, and as they manifested their belief that he would organize a worldly kingdom, and liberate the country from the yoke of the Romans, Jesus instructed and teached them to the contrary; but he perceived that it was necessary to repair to the solitude, that the people should no more believe that his kingdom was of this world, but believe in his words and doctrines as the word of God.

And before night Jesus went to Jerusalem, accompanied by his confidential disciples. But the high council had already sent out many secret messengers to circulate false rumors, and take Jesus a captive. But he was warned and protected by the Essene brethren. He was now very faint and weak, his wounds began again to pain him, and his face was pale. When Jesus entered the city with Peter and John, his friends conducted him into a solitary house, where he called to him the elder of the Essene order. He said that his time for rest was near, and instructed them to wait for him at the "Olive Mount," and thence accompany him to the solitude. Then he gathered his disciples, went through the city and out of the gate that leads to the valley of Jehoshaphat. And his soul was greatly moved, and his heart was sad, as this would be his last walk. Arriving at Kidron, he stopped and wept over Jerusalem. Thence he went further in silence, and his disciples followed him.

And Jesus conducted them to the place he most liked, near the summit of Mount Olive, where can be seen almost the whole "Palestine," for Jesus wanted once more to look upon the country where he had lived and worked. To the east was seen "Jordan," the Dead Sea, and the Arabian mountains; and to the west shone the fires from the temple rock; but on the other side of the mountain was Bethania situated.

And the chosen disciples believed that he would conduct them to Bethania. But the elders of the brotherhood had silently come together on the other side of the mountain, ready to travel, waiting with Jesus, as had been agreed upon.

And he exhorted his disciples to be of good cheer, and firm in their faith; and the more he spoke, his voice grew more and more solemn, and his mind was absorbed in melancholy transport. He prayed for his friends that he had to leave, lifted his arms and blessed them. And the mist rose around the mountain, tinted by the descending sun. Then the elders of the Essene brethren sent word to Jesus that they were waiting, as it was late. And as the disciples knelt down, their faces bent to the grass, Jesus hastily rose and went away through the gathering mist; and when the disciples rose, there stood before them two of our brethren in the white garb of our brotherhood, and they instructed them not to wait for Jesus, as he was gone, whereupon they hastened away down the mountain.

But the disappearance of Jesus filled the disciples

with new hope and confidence, for now they knew that they themselves were to proclaim the word of Jesus, as he, their beloved, would return no more. Therefore they kept faithfully together, and went daily to the temple and the places where he had teached, and the enemies dared not molest them.

But in the city the rumor came out that Jesus was taken up in a cloud, and gone to heaven. This was invented by the people that had not been present when Jesus departed. The disciples did not contradict this rumor, as it served to strengthen their doctrine, and influenced the people who wanted a miracle for to believe in him.

But John, who was present, knew all about it, but he has not spoken nor written anything about it. Likewise Matthew. There are others who have gathered the rumors thereof into an illustration, that they believed themselves as they were moved by the spirit to glorify Jesus. Thus one of them by name of Marcus wrote to a congregation in Rome and gave an account of this event, but as he had not been present, his source was only the rumors among the people. Even thus is it with Lucas, who tried to do the same. But the disciples were advised by the Essene brethren to assume the customs and manners of the Essenes for the sake of unanimity. Therefore they formed a society in which even the women took an officious part, especially Mary and her friends from Galilee.

But Jesus was accompanied on his way by the elders of the brotherhood, likewise Joseph and Nicodemus, and in the night they had to get a beast of burden for Jesus, who grew (very) faint. His mind was greatly moved by taking leave of his friends, and he felt that his death would soon be.

When they at the end of their journey had arrived to the Essene brethren by the "Dead Sea," Jesus was much suffering, and had to be taken care of by the physicians. Joseph and Nicodemus remained with him for several days, and having heard his wishes in lengthy conversations, they took leave of him, promising to inform him minutely about the affairs of the congregations in Jerusalem.

But in Jerusalem none knew that Jesus had returned to the solitude of the order except John and Matthew, to prevent the people from proclaiming him their worldly king. But Joseph and Nicodemus had three times been with him in his place of concealment. On their return they informed us of him. But his body was not vigorous enough to overcome the sufferings he had passed through for want of rest. His soul longed for his disciples, and he was anxious that nothing should be neglected. His restless mind found no consolation in the solitude, and his anxiety consumed his vital power.

But Joseph and Nicodemus had been with him the last time when the sixth full moon was waning, and they came to our brotherhood as we were preparing to partake of the feast of love, and revealed the secret to the elder of our order. And their hearts were sorely grieved, for the chosen one was taken up into the heavenly dwellings of the father. The eternal spirit had quietly bursted the clay, and tranquil as his life was his death. And he was buried by the physician close by the "Dead Sea," as bids the regulations of our brotherhood. But Nicodemus enjoined silence about the death of his friend to all who did not belong to the highest degree.

Here, my dear brethren, you have the only true account of our friend, whom God had called to teach wisdom and virtue to the people through parables and noble deeds. It is now a long time passed since, and the Jews have seven times eaten the passover when I now write this for your information. Thus you can judge for yourselves of the truth of the tradition as it is told by the people.

For I know that many of his new disciples report of miracles, even as they themselves have wished it. And the judicious do not contradict them, because the people is not yet enlightened enough to conceive the truth without supernatural additions. As you yourself have conceived, there are many rumors come from Rome that I need not contradict, for you know yourselves what a brother of our order has to do and not to do. But not only the Jews report superhuman things about him that they believe, but also the Romans, for the pagans believe in gods, and these are identified with the miracles told by the Jews.

And I give you the power to inform the elders of our brotherhood in your parts what I have written to you, but not the novices nor the other degrees. For his is the glory, the son of God, whom we all worship more than the others who are removed to heaven.

And what Jesus has taught while he lived we ought to promote with good will. For he has explained the doctrine minutely to everybody, and to the best of his ability. He has revealed the secret, therefore receive everybody friendly who is called by his name, for his disciples will go to all countries, and you will recognize them by their greeting that is the same as our orders. And you ought to assist them as our brotherhood in Jerusalem and the whole country has served the son of the heavenly father.

This is what I have to say. And just as it is written thus it has passed, for the elders of our brother-hood have witnessed it themselves, and my own eyes have seen him and my ears heard him, and I am a friend of Joseph who sits in the grand council. And forward to the brethren the greeting. Peace be with you.

ADDENDUM

Dear Reader: Now that you have read both of these books, it is most sincerely hoped that, aside from the interest reading, you will have reached several important conclusions: first, that Jesus was not the supernatural man, as has been so presented in the biblical Testaments, nor is he to be confused or compounded with past or present christian religious orthodoxies which link him as the proponent and mainstay with the old pagan Jehovan god, and such more recent contemporary christianities which attempt to redefine Jehovah as the supreme being or, Jesus, his only son, or other definitives, the true facts as have been repeatedly explained in the Unarius texts and now verified in these revelations by Alexander Smyth.

It was the purpose and mission of Jesus to teach a true and factual concept of life, a more relative understanding of creation or the "Father", or as Infinite Intelligence; and by replacing the coercive intimidating, superstitious fears with this practical life-reality, Jehovah would disappear from the mind and heart. Thus, as He said, "Believest thou in Me and thou shalt have eternal life", and which quite clearly defines this belief, not in the personal idiom as a son of god, a supposed "savior" or intercessor, but to believe in what he taught, the true, personally-responsible evolutionary path-way into the heavenly Mansions.

As you have read in the foregoing book, there is much to refute the arch-villainy of those religionists and who, with certain ulterior motivations, contrived to warp, distort, and blaspheme the great and incontestable true facts of life as they were taught and preached by the Nazarene. And in these preachments from his lips will you, as do all other students, find an exact parallel. Yes, in some cases almost the exact wording as in the Unariun texts. You will also conclude, as has been postulated by the Unarius Moderator (E. L. Norman), that there were no miracles per se, as they were described in the Testaments; that the descriptions of these miracles so described are at least, gross exaggerations and in some instances, outright fabrications, purposely written by those who would enslave the minds of the readers. Yes, there were miracles, many of them—not as they were so biblically portrayed but as they are now brought about through the present-day Unarius dispensation; and here again, a great parallel. And there are many other parallels, as they have been previously described, and are best known to those who know something of the Unarius Moderator and his present earth-life. And as one more clinching piece of evidence that, as of to date, readers are reporting the same transcending power, the drowsiness, etc., as they read the book—a characteristic of Unarius, clearly indicating the Unariun Brotherhood were most largely responsible for its appearance upon the earth; and there is no doubt the entire effort was directed and so polarized by the "Unariun Brotherhood on the Inner" who aided those (Saul and Judas) who gave the transcripts.

In face of all this overwhelming mass of evidence, there is only one logical conclusion to be drawn: that Jesus, the Nazarene, and the Unarius Moderator—the Elder Brother, (Ernest L. Norman)—are one and the same, again re-proving and with close parallel lines, the entire Unarius curriculum as an extension and a continuation of the mission of Jesus, and which is most rightfully so; and with certain advantages under the present-day idiom of existing scientific technocracy, also to enable those directly concerned with the crucifixion to work out their karma incurred in that happening.

There is more, much more which could be added to the purposes of the Unarius curriculum; however, these have been served elsewhere. There are two more explanations necessary which will clear away any seeming discrepancies in these two books, as these two books were written at widely divergent times and by different authors. One deals specifically with the life of Jesus from birth to the crucifixion, a life filled with human interest, love and understanding, as well as all other human attributes and proclivities not related in the Testaments.

The true birth of Jesus, his love for Mary (Lazarus' daughter), as childhood sweethearts as they grew up together is one of tremendous romantic appeal, yet here, there should be some clarification with his birth.

During the reign of Herod I, appointed governor by Caesar, it was not the purpose or desire of the Roman governorship to overrule or destroy the Jewish religion, as it was not only the religion of the people but the head priest, Caiaphas, was also the judge and jury, the lawmaker over all important crimes and juris-

dictions relative to the Israeli people. Therefore, to maintain at least a token authority, a lieutenant was appointed by Herod to accompany Caiaphas and sit with him on the stone bench in all matters of judgement; and it was to this position of lieutenant-judge that Herod appointed his own son, Herod Antipas. It was through this constant companionship with Caiaphus in public appearances that Antipas sometimes became known as a priest, and through common usage, his name corrupted to Annanias. It was this same Herod Antipas (Annanias), who seduced and ravaged Glaphira, Princess of Iturea, later known as Hester, the Sybil of Scopus, who, finding she had become pregnant, fled into hiding, taking with her Herod Antipas' gift, the two bracelets.

As this disgrace became a family affair, it quite naturally became the sworn objective of father Herod, number 1, to rid himself of the stigma of an illegitimate child, which resulted in the attempted slaying of the firstborn babes in the province of Judea, City of Bethlehem, where Glaphira was believed to be hiding. Thus it was, that the maiden Mary, Jesus' foster-mother was given the child and who, with the foster-father, the old man, Joseph, reared this son into adulthood, spending part of his early lifetime with the Essenic brotherhood, and in the temple, as described in the book.

The second explanation deals specifically with the crucifixion and to that point where Hester (The Sybil) had left Herod and raced on her horse to the Hill Golgotha where—according to the account as it was described by Alexander—in the twilight hour, she saw Jesus hanging on the cross. According to the account of the crucifixion in the second book, however, finding Jesus still on the cross at this hour would not be entirely accurate—an unaccountable error—but no doubt brought about either in translating the vision or in editing and printing the book. It was the custom, at sundown, to remove any bodies either alive or dead to prevent the obvious purposes of friends and relatives in any rescue efforts. Before removing them, however, the centurions always broke the leg-bones of the victims to defeat any possible escape in case they were still alive; then they would be taken down from the cross and confined in a nearby guard house until the following day when they would again be replaced upon the cross. It has been said that some very hardy victims survived as long as three days. The travail of Jesus lasted seven hours. He was crucified just before noon and taken down at sunset, as it has been depicted in the second book. His body, as was the custom, had been purchased, yet because of the guilt of Pilate and Herod, no monies had been accepted, and as you have read, aroused the suspicions of Caiaphas, etc.

At this point it should be noted that many of the important facts set forth in these two books, names, incidents, etc., were known to the Moderator for many years; in fact, he has spent a lifetime living in much the same manner and form as did Jesus. He has had, in this present lifetime, a most important workout with Caiaphas—also reincarnate in this lifetime—and it was through this workout the Moderator incurred the psychic stigma of nail holes in the palms of his hands, which he still carries. There is also one other episode which should be recounted at this time, even though these, too, will be included in the future biography. It was in April, 1939, the Moderator was taken to the hospital for an emergency appendectomy. While making the customary incision on the right side, the surgeons were astonished to see water issuing from the incision. Before completing the operative procedure, they removed a pint of what they called clear, straw-colored fluid from the abdominal-viscera. This was an unprecedented happening, and so far as could be determined, had never happened before in medical history! Also an attempted laboratory analysis yielded nothing. The fluid could not be analyzed. And so the puzzled doctors were forced to make an entry on the chart as simply, straw-colored fluid.

How exactly similar to that long-ago time when a Roman Centurion, with a spear instead of a surgeon with his scalpel, made an incision into the right side and there, at that time, as recounted in the Testaments and in this book, there issued forth not blood but water. It should also be noted that following the surgery the Moderator, when regaining consciousness, felt and knew there was a large part of him missing—that he was not all there, even though consciousness was normal, and there was, to others apparently nothing amiss.

Two days and two nights later at two A.M., he awakened from sleep, and a moment later had the distinct and clear impression that he had "come back" into his body; and, feeling whole again, he mentally remarked to himself, "Now I'm all here again, I can go back to sleep." How exactly similar was this period of time to that other time when his body lay in the tomb while he hovered *between life and death in another world!*

Shortly after leaving the hospital, the Moderator began to astonish people with his clear and accurate accounts of their past and present lifetimes, as well as their futures.

There was no doubt, somehow during and after that operation, he had been completely reborn! There was an entirely different person now living through and in the body! So great was the difference and so completely incompatible to his wife and friends that he was completely alienated from his past (present) physical life; and shortly after (one year), the complete separation had taken place. He moved to another part of the city, and it was at that time he began to go into the churches, dance halls, private and public gatherings of all kinds, stopping strangers on the street, talking to them in cafes, bus stations, and under any and all conditions he would, to these total strangers, call them by name, mention their addresses, give them information and anecdotes from their past and known only to themselves, information on the future, and sometimes warnings on impending sickness or disasters; and always would these people be transcended with a great healing power. They would accept the blessing and the phenomena without question and go their way, often without so much as a mention to any other person.

In the biography to come, there will be detailed and accurate descriptions of many of these events, and here again there is brought into sharp focus, that with more than fifteen years of very actively deploying himself some sixteen hours a day in giving these clairvoyant and healing demonstrations, displaying an unheard of capacity of this extra-terrestrial phenomena! Strangely enough, he attracted no attention. He did not become a public figure, a well-known Messiah, etc., which bespeaks of the great protection which he and the Unariun Brothers had built around him. For, indeed, it would never be again as it was on the Hill of Golgotha, nor would any chain of circumstances lead to some publicity and recognition which would bring down the wrath and hellish-vindictiveness of the religionists.

For again, as it was in the long ago, this was the same mission, the same purpose to overthrow the Jehovan god, to begin to free men's minds, hearts and souls from the coercive tyranny of these false religions. The Moderator has also very graphically and sometimes dramatically expressed and displayed a parallel clairvoyant aptitude similar to that of Jesus; and from almost all of the years of his present earth life to the present moment, to many thousands of people, gave extremely accurate descriptions of past and present life incidents, and many times accurately foretelling the future twenty years in advance. He has also looked into the past lives of thousands and given accurate descriptions of previous incarnations, often locating as psychic shocks from these lives the true causes of the individual's present-day mental and physical aberrations.

This he has done, as did the Nazarene, under any and all conditions, and always where these psychic demonstrations so manifest, were they also attended by miracles, mental and physical healing, adjustments; and all problems relative to any individual's life were also dissolved. Thus he has done, much of which can be proven, and which he is doing in the present and will continue to do into the future, so long as a humanitarian cause exists.

It is also of very great importance to note that Ruth, beloved wife and right-arm of the earth mission of Unarius, is actually Mary, the childhood playmate and later the espoused of Jesus— an incontestable fact, which can be proven in many ways by her complete love, dedication and understanding. It was Ruth who, at the beginning, without previous training, learned and demonstrated instant typing, sat down to a typewriter and with blanked-out keys, her fingers propelled by unseen hands, flew over the keys unwilled and undirected by her own mind, printed the first pages of the new books. She has also, during the past several years, carried with her the same transcending-healing Power which befuddles clerks in shops and stores and manifests in many ways during the day's activity.

Several students have also, at times, carried this same Power to other people, and while in their presence, became drowsy or felt some other manifestation of power, all of which adds up the total overwhelming proof of all factors of the Unariun Mission!; the thousands of years preparation by both the millions of Unariun Brotherhood, the preparation and conditioning of those persons who would reincarnate to work out and absolve the sin and guilt incurred in the crucifixion, as well as other lifetimes.

Incontestable proof, these Advanced Spiritual Beings, the Unarius Brotherhood do walk with, project Power to aid and abet

101

these Unariun students who have become projective-polarizing agencies.

To Ruth then, goes the fullest measure of appreciation. Her life lived with the Nazarene was one of a number, and through the unending ages of time, stretches back to the sands of an Aegean sea, a temple beside the Nile; the flaming orb of Atlantis; even to the time of Lemuria and the ten lost tribes, remnants of which, as Polynesians, live in the shadows of volcanoes in their South Sea islands. It is part of the background in this present life of the Moderator, who searched for Ruth more than fifteen years before he found her at a most propitious moment, surrounded by the three Wise Men, who had followed him for more than five years. It was during this search that he often described her to friends or even the casual passerby.

Also during this search period, on a number of occasions, he described the house in which he now lives, but which would not be built for many years later. How incredibly wonderful then it is, that through knowledge of the laws of life, a selective reincarnation was possible for these two people to bring themselves together in an earth-life, after a time interval of two thousand years, to again reestablish in their love, an extension and regeneration of a mission foiled by the plotting of selfish, narrow-minded bigots. How great is the love and understanding which can bridge the centuries, travel the endless corridors of time, to again and again find a rejoining and a complete unity of heaven and earth.

So be it, to all those who travel their pathway of life in the unity of love which joins all ends into a universal compassion, which can manifest in all worlds and in all planes and elevations of life, not an implacable destiny ordered by some fancied fate, but one well-chosen according to the ordained laws of universal creation—a unity of soul which unites each individual effort with the entire creative effigy of an interdimensional creation.

Let all these purposes be served; let all the attainments be realized, for such is the fabric of immortality.

We, the Unariun Brothers, and in particular, our Moderator and our most helpful and polarizing agency, our sister Ruth, do sincerely believe these two books will help you to clear away the cobwebs of mysticisms and the derelictions of false religions and their expressions, and that with the Unarius liturgies, our projected help

102

and munificent energies, you will be most materially aided to re-formulate and rebuild your life; that you will find in what we have given you, a constant and never-ending source of courage and inspiration to tread the upward path—a pathway still distorted and roughened with the many impediments of the physical earth-life.

And if all these things are well met, then indeed in some future day, we shall all be joined together and live in the House of the Infinite Creator forever!

The Unariun Brotherhood.